Dear Melanie!

The *The* **BIG-ASS BOOK** of Home Décor

Big crafty hugs!

♡ Mark Montano

The BIG-ASS BOOK of Home Décor

MARK MONTANO

Photographs by Auxy Espinoza

Stewart, Tabori & Chang New York

NOTE TO READERS

All activities in this book should be performed with adult supervision. Common sense and care are essential to the conduct of any and all activities described in this book. Neither the author nor the publisher assumes responsibility for any loss, damage, or injuries that may occur, and the author and publisher hereby expressly disclaim any responsibility for any loss, damages, or injuries, however caused. Neither the author nor the publisher endorses any of the products, tools, or services referred to in this book or assumes any responsibility for use of any such products, tools, or services. All trademarks of products are property of their respective owners. Be sure to follow and read all instructions and warnings that accompany any products, tools, or services referred to in this book. Due to differing conditions, materials, and skill levels, the authors and publisher disclaim any liability for unsatisfactory results. Nothing in this book is intended as an express or implied warrant of suitability or fitness of any product, tool, service, or design.

Published in 2010 by Stewart, Tabori & Chang
An imprint of ABRAMS

Text copyright © 2010 by Mark Montano
Photographs copyright © 2010 by Auxy Espinoza

Library of Congress Cataloging-in-Publication Data:
Montano, Mark.
  The big-ass book of home decor / Mark Montano ; photographs by Auxy Espinoza.
      p. cm.
  Includes index.
  ISBN 978-1-58479-825-5
  1. House furnishings—Amateurs' manuals. 2. Interior decoration—Amateurs' manuals. I. Title.
  TX311.M66 2010
  645—dc22

                    2009036376

Editor: Dervla Kelly
Designer: Anna Christian
Production Manager: Tina Cameron

The text of this book was composed in Aaux.

Printed and bound in China
10 9 8 7 6 5 4 3

Stewart, Tabori & Chang books are available at special discounts when purchased in quantity for premiums and promotions as well as fundraising or educational use. Special editions can also be created to specification. For details, contact specialsales@abramsbooks.com or the address below.

THE ART OF BOOKS SINCE 1949

115 West 18th Street
New York, NY 10011
www.abramsbooks.com

CONTENTS

Perfection is overrated! That's my motto. I don't want to be perfect and I don't expect anything I make or do to be perfect. I think that would be a tragic bore. Instead I like the flaws that make people and things special and give them soul. That's what this book is about . . . perfect imperfection, or as I like to say, being *perfectly imperfect*. When you tackle the crafts in this book, think about a few different things besides the end result. Think about how great it is to be creative, how wonderful it is that you're making something with your own two hands. Mostly, think about the fact that when you make a project it will be unique in the entire world because you made it. If you really don't like it, give it to someone who does, or just start over. (Better yet, give it to someone you don't like and make them display it!) Either way, embrace your creativity and don't be afraid to be *perfectly imperfect*.

If you ever have a question or just want some advice, contact me at markmontanonyc@aol.com.

A big crafty hug to each and every one of you,

*Mark
montano*

PROJECT POINTERS

Here are some guidelines to make your crafting go smoothly and safely. Allow plenty of time to set up your work space and gather the appropriate materials.

BE SAFE

FACE MASK   Make sure to work outdoors or in an extremely well-ventilated area when you use spray paint, and cover your face with a mask to avoid inhaling fumes.

GOGGLES   When working with power tools or sharp materials like glass, always—and I mean always!—wear eye goggles. Use goggles that cover your entire eye area, not just safety glasses.

GLOVES   If you're handling potentially dangerous materials like glass or mirror pieces, it's just common sense to wear gloves. You may want to wear them when working with wire too.

PROTECT YOUR ASSETS

DISHWARE   Whether you've embellished your dishes with decoupage or paint, always hand wash them with warm soapy water and a soft sponge—never put them in the dishwasher.

TABLETOPS   For heavy projects like those made of plaster, make sure to put sticky felt on the bottom of the object to prevent scratching your tabletops.

WORK SPACE   Cover your work space with newspaper before painting, working with plaster, or using glues and adhesives. After all, cleanliness is next to craftiness!

USE THE RIGHT STUFF

I often suggest specific products when I write about crafting. That's because I craft all day and I know what works best. I've tried it all, and I've tossed tons of materials in the trash—glues that didn't hold, paints that dripped or smeared, and other products that for one reason or another just didn't provide the quality a good crafter deserves. So, if you can, stick to the materials listed for the best results, OK? Here are a few of my favorite products.

BENJAMIN MOORE PAINTS   I use Benjamin Moore paints for all my home décor projects because they're simply the best! The paint's quality, the range of colors, and the way it covers are just wonderful. I suggest specific colors for certain projects, but feel free to use whatever suits your fancy.

KRYLON SPRAY PAINTS   For beauty of color, variety of finishes, quick drying time, and durability, you can't go wrong with Krylon. Their Fusion line adheres even to plastic, and their metallic paints are gorgeous. For a mirror-like surface, check out their Looking Glass paint—it's fantastic!

ELMER'S GLUES   For so many crafting projects, Elmer's products are the glue that holds everything together. The classic Elmer's Glue-All and Wood Glue are musts for every home—and every DIYer—and their Craft Bond Spray Adhesive is great for crafters.

MINWAX FINISHES   To add a fine finishing touch to home décor projects from lampshades to tables, you can't do better than Minwax Polycrylic. In spray form or paintable, water-based or oil-based, satin or high gloss, this is good stuff that will protect your projects.

FISKARS SCISSORS   Fiskars scissors for fabric or paper are a really worthwhile investment for crafters. I particularly like their pinking shears, as well as their non-stick scissors, which allow you to cut sticky things without the glue adhering to the blades.

AMAZING GOOP GLUES   "Glues whatever. Bonds forever." That's what the company claims for Amazing Goop Household glue and E-6000, and it's true! I should know—I use them for just about every project that requires a really strong adhesive. I love my Goop!

For a list of other products and companies that will make crafting a breeze, see the resource list starting on page 266.

CHAPTER 1

DELICIOUS DINNERWARE

If you're setting a table, **you should have something pretty cool to accent your terrific chairs and dining room**, right? I've been hitting the 99¢ store pretty regularly since I wrote *Dollar Store Décor*. I find you can grab the **coolest items** there for your craft projects at a fraction of what they might cost somewhere else. The clear glass plates are my absolute favorite purchases. **Creating decorative plates and beautiful dishes has become an obsession.** I'll make dishes for friends to **celebrate** special occasions or just to **match** a new tablecloth. Try photocopying fabric and using small images from it for a set of plates. Copy an image of the queen and superimpose a photo of your dear friend to **make a commemorative plate** for her birthday. How about taking a family photo and using it for **a set of family dinnerware**? The possibilities are endless, and I guarantee you'll have as much fun making these plates as I do. A good friend of mine put a saying on the underside of her set: "Congratulations, you have finished your plate and now you get to do the dishes!" I thought it was brilliant. My set is going to say, "If you can read this, then you really are a good friend because I'm a terrible cook. Oh, I'm sorry if your tummy hurts!" However you decide to alter your dinnerware, once you're done, **always carefully hand wash your new and improved dishes**—never put them in the dishwasher.

CIRCLE AND SQUARE GLASS PLATES

The great thing about glass plates is that you can decorate their undersides and still eat off of them safely. I pick mine up everywhere, from thrift stores to 99¢ stores, and they make the best craft projects. Think about making special plates to match your kitchen or to celebrate a special occasion (e.g., hearts for Valentine's Day or spades for a poker tournament). The possibilities are endless!

YOU'LL NEED:

Contact paper

Scissors

Glass plates, in any size from 8" to 14" in diameter

Newspaper

Krylon Fusion spray paint in 2 colors (preferably 1 light and 1 dark for contrast)

Minwax Polycrylic Protective Finish

1"-wide paintbrush

To make plates with a square design, follow the instructions here, but cut squares instead of circles from the contact paper.

HERE'S HOW:

1. Fold a piece of contact paper in half and cut out a half-circle about 7" in diameter along the fold. The circle doesn't have to be perfect—it can even be oblong.

2. Keep the contact paper folded and, following the arc of the first cut, carefully trim off ½" to make a ring.

3. Continue to cut concentric half-circles until you get to the straight edge of the folded paper.

4. Unfold the largest circle, peel off the protective backing, and place the sticky side of the paper on the back of the plate.

5. Skipping the next size, peel off the protective backing of the next smallest circle and put it in the center of the first circle.

6. Skip another size, then peel and stick the next smallest circle in the center of the last one. Continue this way with the remaining circles.

7. If you like, you can follow steps 1 to 6 with a second piece of contact paper, sticking it to another part of the plate.

8. Put the plate face down on newspaper outdoors. Spray it with one of your colors. (I like to start with the dark color.) Use several coats of paint, letting it dry for 10 minutes between coats so you get nice coverage.

9. When it's dry, flip the plate over to check for any missed spots.

10. Carefully peel off the circles and spray paint the back with the second color. It will fill in the parts where the contact paper circles were before. Use several coats of this color, waiting at least 10 minutes between coats.

11. When the paint is completely dry, brush the back of the plate with at least two coats of Polycrylic, waiting at least 20 minutes between coats.

COMIC-BOOK PARTY

Getting older? How about some comic relief? I'm a huge fan of comics, and I always have been. I love the colors, the stories, and the little bubbles with exclamations like POW! BOOM! ZAP! and my all-time favorite, BLAM! No matter how much of a girly boy I was as a child, I still wanted to be Aquaman. This was probably because of the outfit more than anything, but he was really cool! Roy Lichtenstein brought comics images into pop art, and now I'm bringing them to party accessories. These plates and coasters, super easy to make, are a perfect gift for the birthday boy or girl when the party is over.

Look for comics you can cut up or enlarge on a copy machine. For you Mac users, the newer computers have a program called Comic Life that lets you make your own comics from your computer—check it out!

YOU'LL NEED:

To make the plates:

Comic books for copying

Scissors

Wite-Out

Computer to print out your sayings (or a black pen)

1"-wide paintbrush

Elmer's Glue-All

Glass plates

Lace, nylon athletic fabric, or a fabric with lots of holes

Krylon Spray Adhesive

Newspaper

Krylon Fusion spray paint in 2 or 3 flat colors (I used red, blue, and yellow)

Minwax Polycrylic Protective Finish (semigloss or high gloss)

Masking tape

HERE'S HOW:

To make the plates:

1. Cut out a comic-book panel that you think would work well.

2. Use Wite-Out to cover up the wording.

3. On a color copy machine, enlarge the image to the size you need: 4" square will work for both the plates and the coasters.

4. Type out the sayings you'd like to include in the bubbles, print and cut them out, and paste them onto the image with glue. (Or simply write them in neatly with black pen.) Make them funny! Create extra bubbles for birthday or other greetings.

5. With a paintbrush, spread Elmer's glue on the face of the image and adhere it to the back of the plate so it shows on the front.

6. Cut out a circle of the lace or fabric at least as large as the plate. Spray it with the adhesive and press it on the back of the plate, making sure that it sticks onto the entire surface.

7. Lay the plate face down on newspaper and spray the back with the first color of paint. Wait about 10 minutes, then carefully remove the lace.

8. Spray the back of the plate with the second color of paint, filling in where the lace was.

Instructions continue on next two pages.

9. *Optional:* You'll notice that on page 16 one of the plates has half one color and half another color—this is really easy to do!

a. With the lace (or other holey material) over the back of the plate, cover up part of the plate with tape and newspaper and spray the uncovered part with the first paint color. Let dry for 10 minutes.

b. Remove the paper, cover the painted part of the plate with tape and paper, and spray the uncovered part with the second paint color. Let dry for 10 minutes.

c. Remove the lace and spray the entire plate with at least two coats of the third paint color, waiting 10 minutes between coats.

10. When the plate is completely dry, paint over the back several times with the Polycrylic, waiting 20 minutes between coats. Then let dry for 24 hours.

To make the coasters:

Comic books for copying

Scissors

Wite-Out

Computer to print out your sayings (or a black pen)

1"-wide paintbrush

Elmer's Glue-All

4" squares of ¼"-thick birch plywood OR a set of coasters from the 99¢ store to use as a base

Elmer's Painters pen with chisel tip in black

Sticky felt or ultrasuede

To make the coasters:

1. Make your images the same way you did for the plates in a 4"-square size (steps 1 to 4 above).

2. Paint the Elmer's glue on the back of the image and adhere it to the wood block (or the purchased coasters).

3. With the black paint pen, draw around the edges to give the coaster a nice finished look.

4. Put the coasters face down on a flat surface and spray paint the backsides with one of the colors from the plates.

5. When they're dry, flip them right side up and apply several coats of the Polycrylic on the coasters. Start with a very thin coat and let it dry, then slowly build up layers and let them dry between coats.

6. Cut out sticky felt the size of the coaster and adhere it to the back of the coaster. BOOM! BAM! ZAP! You're ready to party!

Safety Note: Always spray paint outdoors, and wear a face mask to avoid inhaling fumes.

MULTICOLOR STRIPED GLASS PLATES

I'm a freak for multicolor anything—shoes, plates, hair, you name it. If it has a million colors, I'm all over it like feathers on a duck. These plates could possibly be my most favorite of all the plates I've ever made, and honey, I've made some plates in my time. So stripe it up, kiddos, and join me on this multistripe plate-making adventure!

YOU'LL NEED:

1"-wide blue painter's tape

Glass plates

Craft knife

Krylon Fusion spray paint in at least 6 different colors

Newspaper

Minwax Polycrylic Protective Finish

1"-wide paintbrush

HERE'S HOW:

1. Apply a piece of painter's tape all the way across the back of one edge of your plate. Make sure it's really stuck on there—you don't want any bubbles.

2. Next to the first piece of tape, and overlapping it a tiny bit, place another piece of tape.

3. Continue this way until you've covered the entire plate except for the last little stripe on the opposite edge.

4. Cut off any excess tape around the edge of the plate with a craft knife.

5. Line up your spray paints in the order in which you want the stripes to appear on the plate. Lay the plate, tape side up, on newspaper outdoors.

6. Spray the little uncovered stripe with your first color and wait about 5 minutes.

7. Remove the first piece of tape, spray another color, and wait 5 minutes.

8. Remove another piece of tape, spray a third color, and wait 5 minutes.

9. Continue until the entire plate is painted.

10. With your last color, coat the entire back of the plate.

11. When your plate is dry, paint on several coats of Polycrylic, waiting about 20 minutes between coats, and then let dry for 24 hours.

BUTTERFLY PLATES

These plates are obviously an homage to Gianni Versace, who loved both bright colors and butterflies. I like them because they are chic and punk at the same time. The technique for these plates is really easy to master and you can use almost any image, so have fun and make an entire table setting.

YOU'LL NEED:

Images of butterflies for copying onto bright paper

Scissors

Elmer's Glue-All

1"-wide paintbrush

Glass plates

Newspaper

Krylon Fusion spray paint in black

Minwax Polycrylic Protective Finish

HERE'S HOW:

1. Copy your images on bright-colored paper. I dig the fluorescent colors that you can find at Staples.

2. Cut out the images, retaining as much detail as you can.

3. Using the brush, paint a light coat of glue onto the face of the image. Adhere the image to the back of the plate so you can see it from the front.

4. Continue to add butterflies until you're satisfied with your design.

5. When the images are dry, wipe off the excess glue from around the edges to make sure the plate is clean.

6. Lay the plate face down on newspaper outdoors.

7. Spray on the black paint until the plate is completely covered.

8. When the paint is dry, coat the back of the plate with at least 2 coats of Minwax, waiting at least 20 minutes between coats, and then let dry for 24 hours.

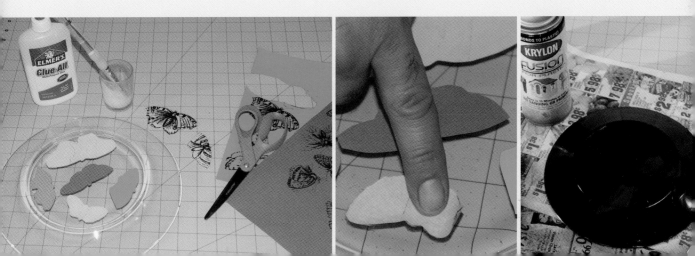

CHAPTER 2

PERFECT PILLOWS

I don't know how you feel about pillows, but **I think they are the jewelry of the home.** Nothing brings more life to a boring sofa or plain bedding than a fantastic pillow that screams style. **It's the exclamation point on your furniture!** The cherry on top! I have to admit I'm someone who changes my pillows as often as I change my underwear (at least once a week—*I'm kidding!*). But let's be serious for a minute. You can't have the same pillow on your sofa for winter, spring, summer, and fall! And what if you get a **fantastic** new throw? Will your pillows match? Really, there are so many things to consider. Here's how I work it out: I just make pillows 'til the cows come home. **I get an idea and I make a pillow.** I find two yards of a fabric I love and I make a pillow. I design a new stencil and I make a pillow. I'm simply a compulsive pillow maker. It's so much easier—and cheaper—to change the look of a sofa by adding new pillows than by sewing a whole new slipcover. I hope these ideas inspire you to **create your own pillows using things you have around the house** or using trims in a new way.

HARLEQUIN PILLOW

If you thumb through this book, chances are you'll notice that my favorite pattern is harlequin and my second favorite is leaves. It's not that I don't love other patterns—these just sing to me. While working on my harlequin wall technique it occurred to me that it might be fun to sponge-paint some fabric and see how it turned out. It worked, and I'm deeply, madly, incandescently in love with my new green harlequin pillow.

YOU'LL NEED:

Scissors

Cellulose sponge

Hot glue gun and glue stick

Small piece of wood or heavy-duty cardboard at least 2" x 3"

Paint (I used Benjamin Moore house paint, but you can use acrylic or fabric paint)

Plastic plate

Scrap cardboard

Two 15" x 21" pieces of fabric

Sewing machine

Contrasting thread for detail

Fringe to go around edge

Pillow stuffing

Needle with thread that matches the fabric

HERE'S HOW:

1. Decide how big you want your diamonds to be. Mine were 3" high by 2" wide. Cut that shape out of the cellulose sponge.

2. Hot glue the sponge shape onto the small piece of wood or heavy cardboard.

3. Pour out a small amount of paint onto a plastic plate.

4. Dip the sponge stamp in the paint and practice on a piece of cardboard first.

5. When you get the hang of it, start dipping and stamping along the base of one piece of fabric. Do this in a straight line so the side corners of the diamonds are touching. Don't worry about the design being perfect!

6. Continue with the next row, making sure to touch all corners of the diamonds as you go along. Do this until the entire piece of fabric is covered.

7. When the paint is dry, thread your sewing machine with the contrasting thread and stitch straight lines between the diamonds, like you would see in an argyle pattern.

8. With the fringe facing in toward the center of the pillow, stitch it around the edge of the pillow using a ¼" to ⅜" seam allowance.

9. Place the other panel of fabric on top of the painted fabric and stitch them together, trapping the fringe in a ½" seam allowance all the way around and leaving a 5" opening.

10. Clip the corners at an angle and turn the pillow right side out.

11. Fill with pillow stuffing and hand-stitch the opening closed.

For the blue harlequin pillow, follow the instructions above, but skip the contrasting thread and the fringe.

BUTTERFLY DOODLE PILLOW

As much as I love to embroider, it takes forever to make a project I'm happy with. So I decided to take my trusty Kenmore sewing machine for a spin and see what I could come up with using basic stitches and black thread. All I can say is that almost every shirt I own now has a butterfly embroidered on the back. If you don't have a light box for this project, use a lamp under a glass table or a window with light coming through it.

YOU'LL NEED:

Image of a butterfly, dragonfly, etc. for copying (mine is from a Dover clip art book)

Light box

½ yard of white fabric

Pencil

Sewing machine

Black thread

Iron and ironing board

½ yard of black fabric

Pillow stuffing

Sewing needle

HERE'S HOW:

1. Enlarge your image on a copy machine.

2. Place the image on the light box and the white fabric on top of it.

3. Using a pencil, lightly trace the image onto the fabric, keeping in mind that each line you make will be covered with thread.

4. With your sewing machine, slowly go over each penciled line in black thread using a straight stitch. To make the darker areas more interesting, you can go over them with a zigzag stitch to get more thread on the fabric. And don't worry—you can always add more if it's not quite right.

5. When you're finished sewing, iron the fabric.

6. Place the black fabric (for the back of the pillow) facing the white fabric and sew right sides together, leaving a 5" opening for stuffing.

7. Clip the corners at an angle and turn the pillow right side out.

8. Fill with pillow stuffing and hand-stitch the opening closed.

TWISTED-RIBBON PILLOW

I love sewing ribbon onto pillows, but I was kinda getting bored with it. That's when I started to get a little twisted—with ribbon, that is! Instead of sewing the ribbon on completely flat, I decided to twist it as I sewed and add a little texture to my project. I'm warning you: Eventually your ribbon is going to get smooshed and move around a bit. But after a while my pillow started to look like a terrific antique. Just have fun with it—and see how twisted you can get!

YOU'LL NEED:

Pencil

Ruler

Two 14" x 21" pieces of fabric

9 yards of 1"-wide ribbon

Scissors

Sewing machine and thread

Pillow stuffing

Sewing needle

HERE'S HOW:

1. On the first piece of fabric, draw a 21" line lengthwise 5" down from the top and another one 5" up from the bottom. Mark every inch across the 21" sides of the fabric.

2. Cut 19 pieces of ribbon 15" long.

3. Skip the first 1" from the left and, with the sewing machine, stitch on the ribbon pieces all the way across the top using a $\frac{3}{8}$" seam allowance and following the 1" markings.

4. Time to start twisting! Take the first ribbon, twist it once to the right, lay it on the line that's 5" down from the top of the fabric, and stitch.

5. Continue to do this all the way across until you've completed the first line of twisted ribbon.

6. Repeat the process on the next line down, twisting each ribbon to the right and then stitching.

7. Repeat this process once more for the last line of stitching, $\frac{1}{2}$" from the bottom edge. See how easy that was!

8. Place the second piece of fabric over the ribbon and stitch around the edge of the two panels, leaving a 5" opening.

9. Clip the corners at an angle and turn the pillow right side out.

10. Fill with pillow stuffing and hand-stitch the opening closed.

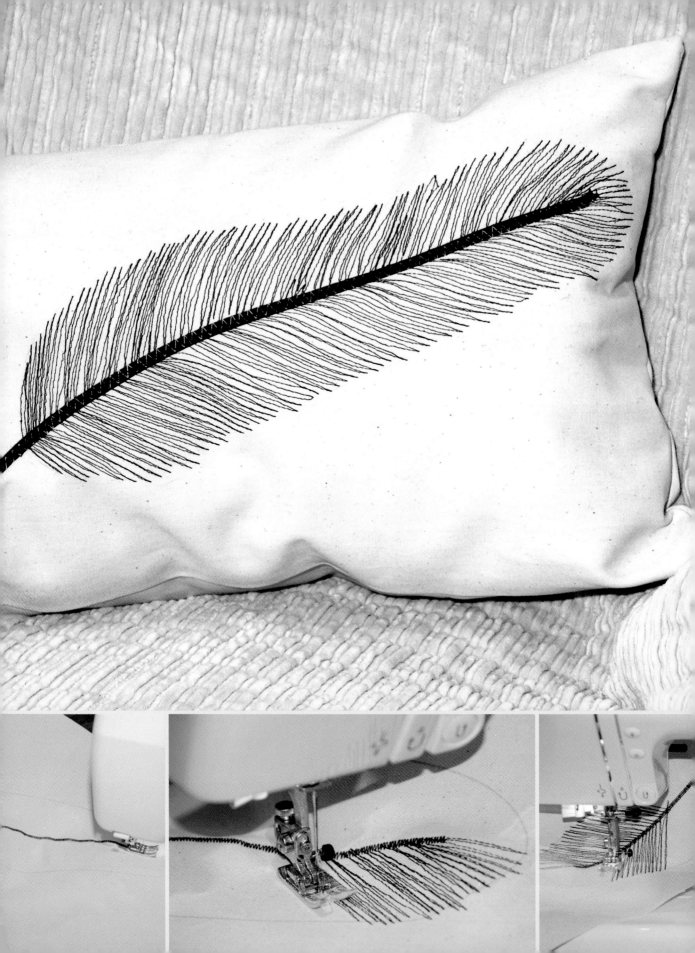

CHIC DOODLE FEATHER PILLOW

Feel like doing some embroidery but think you don't have time? I'm right there with you, so recently I started drawing with my sewing machine. Now I'm addicted! It's relaxing and fun and doesn't take nearly as long as traditional embroidery techniques (which I still love to do when I have the time). This design is simple and chic, and lately I've been putting it on everything from pillowcases to dinner napkins. After you learn this craft we will truly be birds of a feather.

YOU'LL NEED:

1 yard of fabric in black or white (I used canvas)

Scissors

Scrap paper

Pencil

Sewing machine

Thread that contrasts with the fabric (I used black, but brown could be wonderful)

14" piece of ¼"-wide black ribbon (optional)

Pillow stuffing

Sewing needle

Red thread and a 14" piece of red yarn (optional, for the red pillow; see below)

HERE'S HOW:

1. Cut the fabric into two equal rectangles.

2. Draw a feather on scrap paper to determine its size and shape. Lightly pencil the feather on the first piece of fabric.

3. On the sewing machine, zigzag stitch the feather shaft first. This will serve as your guide as you stitch the rest of the feather. If you prefer a more solid line, zigzag stitch over a piece of ribbon to make the shaft.

4. Starting a couple of inches up from the base of the shaft, begin stitching the parallel barbs (fancy description of feather fluff!) on one side of the feather using a straight stitch.

5. Following your light pencil sketch, stitch back and forth from the shaft. Do this all the way up to the top of the shaft and then all the way down the other side. Fill in with additional stitches if you need more "fluff" on the feather.

6. With right sides together, stitch the pillow front to the second piece of fabric around the edges, leaving a 5" opening.

7. Clip the corners at an angle and turn the pillow right side out.

8. Fill with pillow stuffing and hand-stitch the opening closed.

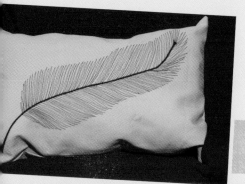

For the red pillow, in step 3, zigzag stitch over a piece of red yarn to make the shaft. Then follow the remaining instructions.

EMBELLISHED IRON-ON-IMAGE PILLOW

If you can make an iron-on design for a T-shirt, why not do it for a pillow? It's easy and looks wonderful. But don't stop there—embellish the images you've chosen and make them POP! If you have an image of a dog, add a collar with a bow. If you have an image of a woman, put a beautiful brooch on her dress. Think of things that will make your pillows unique and wonderful. C'mon, you can do it!

YOU'LL NEED:

1 yard of smooth 100% cotton fabric

Scissors

Images you want to transfer

Computer and printer

Avery T-shirt Transfers for Inkjet Printers (try Staples)

Iron and ironing board

Embellishments (I used 1 yard of 1"-wide ribbon for bows)

Sewing needle and thread

Hot glue gun and glue stick, or fabric glue (optional)

Sewing machine

Pillow stuffing

HERE'S HOW:

1. Decide how big you want your pillow (mine is 14" x 22"), and cut two panels of fabric that size.

2. Following the instructions on the package of iron-on heat-transfer paper, use your computer and printer to print out your chosen images.

3. Iron the images onto one of the fabric panels, again following the instructions on the package.

4. Decide how you want to embellish the images. You can hand-stitch the embellishments onto the pillow to keep them in place, or use a hot glue gun or fabric glue. Hot glue dries quickly; fabric glue takes a bit more time.

5. Use the sewing machine to stitch the pillow front to the other piece of fabric around the edges, with right sides together, leaving a 5" opening.

6. Clip the corners at an angle and turn the pillow right side out.

7. Fill with pillow stuffing and hand-stitch the opening closed.

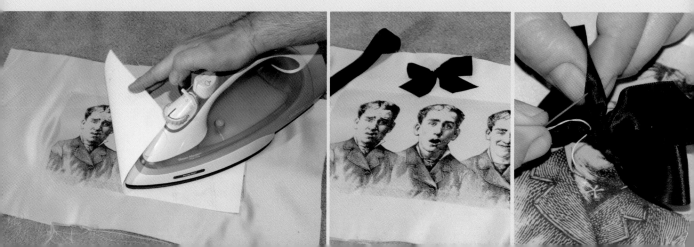

LACE AND HOT GLUE PILLOW

I love hot gluing fabrics together—the bond is just amazing! I found this lace last year at a fabric store and figured I would cut it apart and use the flowers separately to embellish something. Cut to a year later, when I finally sat down to make this pillow in two of my favorite decorating colors, pink and yellow. Any lace will do for a project like this. I think you'll really like the results.

YOU'LL NEED:

1 yard of lace you can cut apart

Scissors

Pillow you want to cover

Dritz Fray Check

Straight pins

Hot glue gun and glue sticks

Sewing needle and thread

HERE'S HOW:

1. Cut the lace apart to separate the flowers and leaves.

2. If the lace has an edge that's rough or may fray, apply Fray Check.

3. Carefully open a seam on the pillow and remove the stuffing.

4. Lay the pillow flat, arrange the lace pieces where you want them, and keep them in place with pins.

5. Use hot glue to attach all the pieces to the pillow.

6. Restuff the pillow and sew the hole closed.

Suggestion: If you're really adventurous, try using this technique all over an old chair that needs sprucing up.

BLUE-PLATE-SPECIAL STENCIL PILLOW

I'm a huge fan of stencils, and there are tons of different ways to make them. These are so easy that once you get the hang of it, you'll be working your magic on everything from T-shirts to pillowcases to curtain panels. Make any shape you want out of contact paper; just start cutting and see what happens!

YOU'LL NEED:

1 yard of 60"-wide canvas or white cotton

Scissors

Ruler

Pen

Plate for tracing circles, 9"–10" in diameter

Contact paper

Newspaper

Krylon Fusion spray paint (I used blue)

Sewing machine and thread

Pillow stuffing

Sewing needle

HERE'S HOW:

1. Cut two 22" x 22" pieces of fabric.

2. With a pen and a ruler, draw a thin cross on one of the pieces, dividing it into four equal sections. In each section, trace around the plate so that the edge of the circle touches the lines you've drawn on both sides.

3. Trace around the plate in the exact center of the fabric.

4. Continue tracing the plate to achieve the design shown on the pillow in the photo. To create the design, all you need to do is intersect the circles evenly. (You will notice perfect "eye" shapes emerging from the pattern.)

5. Create the same pattern on a sheet of contact paper and cut out 16 of the "eye" shapes for the pillow.

6. Stick the shapes to the pillow, following the traced pattern.

7. Cover your outdoor work surface with newspaper. Lay the prepared fabric on the paper.

8. Spray paint the pillow. When it's dry, remove the contact paper.

9. If you'd like to create the pattern on the back of the pillow as well, repeat steps 2 to 8 on the other piece of fabric.

10. Once the paint is dry, stitch right sides of the front and back together, using ½" seam allowance around the edges and leaving a 5" opening.

11. Clip the corners at an angle and turn the pillow right side out.

12. Fill with pillow stuffing and hand-stitch the opening closed.

STRING ART PILLOW

Give me an afternoon and a way to make a cool fabric and I'm there! One of my favorite activities is to wrap something in string and spray paint over it. I did this with the dresser on page 232 and decided to try it with fabric to make a pillow. I think it looks darn modern, and each time you do it the effect will be different. Try using a different color on the front and back of the pillow. Or use this technique on a canvas and make really cool art!

YOU'LL NEED:

Two 16" x 24" pieces of white cotton fabric

16" x 24" piece of cardboard

Ball of yarn

Newspaper

Krylon Fusion spray paint in red

Scissors

Sewing machine and thread

Pillow stuffing

Sewing needle

HERE'S HOW:

1. Place one of the fabric pieces on top of the cardboard.

2. Wrap the yarn around the fabric and cardboard together. Go nuts! The more string and varied directions, the better.

3. When you're done wrapping, put the wrapped fabric on newspaper outdoors and spray paint the whole thing.

4. Wait a few minutes until the paint dries and then cut the string off the pillow.

5. Repeat steps 1 to 4 with the other piece of fabric.

6. When the paint is completely dry, place right sides of the painted fabrics together. Using ½" seam allowance, stitch the two pieces together around the edges, leaving a 5" opening.

7. Clip the corners at an angle and turn the pillow right side out.

8. Fill with pillow stuffing and hand-stitch the opening closed.

BIRDCAGE PILLOW

There is nothing sadder than a real bird in a cage, but I do love a good birdcage print, on either wallpaper or fabric. I also quite like interesting pillows. This kooky pillow was inspired by a fabric print I once saw and decided to imitate. Once you've made the pillow, perch it perfectly in a special place. Neat, sweet, and tweet!

YOU'LL NEED:

Template on page 258

Pencil

8" x 8" piece of contact paper

Craft knife

Hole punch

Two 20" x 15" pieces of white cotton twill fabric

Newspaper

Krylon Fusion spray paint

10" piece of 1"-wide ribbon (I used olive green)

Sewing machine with black thread

6" piece of ¼"-wide ribbon

Pillow stuffing

Sewing needle

HERE'S HOW:

1. Use the template to draw the bird image onto the contact paper and cut it out with a craft knife, putting the bird shape aside.

2. Once you know where you want the bird to be, peel the backing off the remaining contact paper (the part with the bird hole in it) and place it on the fabric, using it as a stencil.

3. Use the hole punch to make a dot for the bird's eye out of contact paper, and stick it in place.

4. Place the fabric on newspaper outdoors and spray paint just the exposed bird shape. Peel off the contact paper when the paint is dry.

5. Sketch birdcage bars and a perch for the bird onto the fabric.

6. Stitch the 1"-wide piece of ribbon about 3" up from the base of the pillow to make the bottom of the birdcage.

7. With your sewing machine and black thread, go over the birdcage lines—like you're sketching with thread.

8. Sew a loop of the ¼" ribbon downward at the top of the cage.

9. Place the painted fabric on top of the other piece of fabric and cut around the design, leaving at least 1" all the way around.

10. Place right sides of the fabric pieces together. Using ½" seam allowance, stitch around the edges, leaving a 5" opening.

11. Clip the corners at an angle and turn the pillow right side out.

12. Fill with pillow stuffing and hand-stitch the opening closed.

CHAPTER 3

WONDERFUL WALLS

I have a fantastic mother who never got angry when we drew on the walls as kids. In fact, she encouraged us to **be creative** in whatever way we wanted. Her solution to child graffiti was to tape **large sheets of butcher paper** to a wall near the floor. We were young and short, and this is where we experimented! Mom's genius idea kept us creating and saved her from having to repaint. When I turned 14, I was allowed to paint whatever I wanted on my bedroom walls. I decided to **hide the pipe in the corner of the room** with a jungle scene complete with monkeys in a huge tree. I also discovered **painter's tape** and geometric shapes. My teenage refuge looked much like what my home looks like now. And it's all because of my terrific mother.

      I still like to be creative with my walls. I'm not a huge fan of wallpaper because my tastes change way too quickly. But even if you're just covering your walls with paint, they don't have to be boring! There are so many great wall treatments you can use. And then you can paint over them, rather than spending hours steaming off paper that doesn't work for you anymore. I've tried things like small pieces of paper adhered to the wall and **hand-painted techniques** that, in a way, echo what wallpaper can do. My favorite technique is a rolling pin with kids' sticky foam patterns stuck to it. I've been able to use this idea in many different ways. **Think of your walls as a huge canvas** and go nuts.

      Warning: When you do something terrific to your walls, you may initially be overwhelmed by either the color or the pattern you've chosen. **Give it a few days.** Put your art back on the wall and live with it for a bit. It may take a little time for you to adjust to the change in your surroundings, but I bet you'll start to love it after a short while.

SILHOUETTE WALL TREATMENT

I love to make walls super special with printed images and hand painting. This wall technique can be used with anything from cut-out flowers to silhouettes of your own family. Check out Dover books for a great selection of images.

YOU'LL NEED:

Benjamin Moore flat wall paint (I used Tropicana Cabana)

Black and white images of an antique silhouette for copying

Scissors

Pencil

Tape measure

Elmer's Glue-All

1"-wide paintbrush

Ruler

Tracing paper (optional, if you're not sure how to paint the ribbons and bows)

Black acrylic paint

Small fine-tipped brush

HERE'S HOW:

1. Paint your wall and let it dry.

2. Print out your chosen silhouettes at a copy center. *Note:* Don't print them from your computer at home because the ink in home printers is water based and will run when you put glue on the paper. You'll need about 60 images for a wall 6' wide by 8' high, so do the math to figure out how many copies you should make. Cut out each image.

3. Using a tape measure, mark the exact center of the wall, where you will place the first image.

4. With a brush, spread Elmer's glue on the back of the image and carefully place it on the wall.

5. Proceeding in a straight line, place the next image 10" directly below the first.

6. Continue this way until you've completed one entire row from top to bottom on the wall.

7. Make the next rows 14" to the left and right of the first row. To create a diamond pattern with the images, position the first image in these new rows exactly halfway between the first and second images in the original row.

8. Using the first images in the new rows as your starting point, mark the position of the following images at 10" intervals down the wall.

9. Follow steps 4 to 6 for each row all the way along the wall.

10. When you've glued all the images on the wall, use tracing paper to practice drawing ribbons and bows.

11. Once you have it down, draw the flourishes freehand on the wall in pencil, then go over the lines with the black paint and small paintbrush.

HARLEQUIN WALL TECHNIQUE

This technique is so easy that once you've tried it, you may want to paint your entire house this way! I've used two different shades of green here, but you could go crazy with color or maybe just use a high-gloss protective finish over a flat paint to give the wall some texture. Think about it!

YOU'LL NEED:

Cellulose sponge

Scissors

Hot glue gun and glue stick

Small pieces of wood

Paint in 2 colors, 1 dark and 1 light (I used Benjamin Moore Jalapeno Pepper and Olive Green, both flat)

Plastic plate

Scrap cardboard

HERE'S HOW:

1. Decide how big you want your diamonds to be. Mine were 3" high by 2" wide. Cut that shape out of the cellulose sponge.

2. Hot glue the sponge onto a small piece of wood.

3. Paint your wall the lighter of the two shades. (In my case it was Jalapeno Pepper.)

4. Once the wall is dry, pour a small amount of the darker paint (Olive Green, in my case) onto a plastic plate.

5. Dip the sponge stamp in the paint and practice on a piece of cardboard.

6. When you feel comfortable with the stamping, start along the base of your wall, dipping and stamping in a straight line so the side corners of the diamonds are touching.

7. Continue with the next row up, making sure all corners of the diamonds touch as you go. If you get to the top or the end of a wall and there isn't enough room for a full diamond, simply cut out the shape you need from the sponge, make it into another stamp, and move right along.

8. Stamp away until the entire wall is covered.

ROLLING PIN PAINT TECHNIQUE

Rolling pins aren't just for smacking wise-cracking kids anymore. I've found a much better use for these piecrust contraptions—and thank goodness. I was about to toss one and then decided to experiment with it. I went to the 99¢ store and picked up a few more, and now I have an entire collection. Watch out, lady, these rolling pins are mine and I'm not afraid to use them!

I like painting paper, walls, and furniture with my rolling pins. You can truly coat any object. Once you've covered your surface using one color, you can go over it with another color to give it some dimension.

YOU'LL NEED:

1 or 2 rolling pins

Measuring tape

Large sheet of paper

Scissors

Pencil

2 sheets of sticky foam

Paint in 1 or 2 colors

Paint tray or flat container

Flat surface for practice (scrap wood, newspaper, cardboard, etc.)

HERE'S HOW:

1. Measure your rolling pin. Mine was 8" around and 11" long.

2. Cut out a piece of paper to that exact size.

3. Draw a neat design on the paper. Use things like leaves, stars, and diamonds or, if you feel confident, go into more complex shapes. Figure out how many shapes you'll need to cut out to cover the rolling pin.

4. Cut the shapes out of the sticky foam, peel off the protective backing, and stick them to the rolling pin following the pattern you drew on the paper.

5. Once you've duplicated your paper design with sticky foam on the rolling pin, give it a whirl! Pour some paint into the paint tray or other flat container. You can use a cookie sheet if you want—it's nice and flat and the rolling pin will fit inside well.

6. As if you were preparing cookie dough, roll the rolling pin in the paint. Practice rolling the paint onto a flat surface (I use large pieces of scrap wood or newspaper). Once you know how the paint will react, you can start rolling the paint on your desired object.

7. Cover the entire surface of your wall or object, let it dry, and then—if you like—repeat steps 1 to 6 with a new rolling pin and a different paint color.

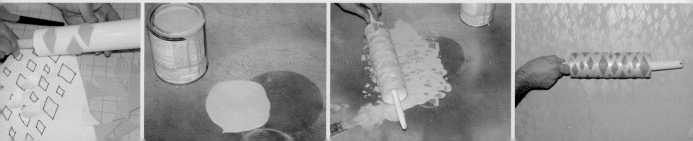

CHAPTER 4

WHIMSICAL WINDOWS

Seems cell phone paparazzi are everywhere these days! Let me explain. The other day I was doing something I've done ever since I've lived alone: **I was vacuuming in the buff.** I can't help it! If the good lady above intended us to vacuum fully dressed, it would have been written somewhere in the big book . . . and I haven't been able to find it. **I've asked a lot of people if they like to clean in the buff, and many have admitted to enjoying it.** OK, let me finish my story. I had cranked some Aretha Franklin, had the vacuum going full blast (I was using the attachments and **getting in all the nooks and crannies**), and was enjoying myself tremendously. When I turned off the vacuum to head into another room, I heard the doorbell ring. I turned toward the front door, horrified, to see a good friend looking directly at me through the window and laughing hysterically. He pointed his cell phone at me, and **I'm afraid he snapped a photo to torture me for the rest of my life.** I screamed, grabbed a pillow from my sofa, and **froze**. Now that all my friends know I clean in the buff, I figured I would share this story with you too. But I want to be clear here—**I'm not ashamed of it.** In fact, I think it's a pretty smart thing to do as long as you're not using heavy equipment.

      The lesson I learned here was simple: Put a window treatment over the front door window. That's all! Drapes, curtains, blinds—we need them to keep our little idiosyncrasies private. I hope these fun window treatments will keep you from ending up as dinner conversation among your friends.

MOROCCAN-INSPIRED STAINED GLASS WINDOW

I don't think I've ever used an office folder for its intended purpose. That's probably why I didn't keep my office jobs for very long—too many art projects at my desk! Colorful office folders make great "stained glass," and here's the proof. Thank you, Staples, for making my desk a source of inspiration once again!

YOU'LL NEED:

For a 26" x 36" window:

Template on page 258

Fine-point permanent marker

12 clear plastic office folders
(3 each in 4 different colors)

Scissors

Elmer's Craft Bond Spray Adhesive

HERE'S HOW:

1. Trace the template shape onto one plastic folder repeatedly, creating the pattern shown on the window in the photo. (The shapes fit together nicely, so you won't have to waste much of the folder.) Cut the pieces out.

2. Repeat this process with the other folders.

3. Clean your window thoroughly.

4. Lightly spray one of the plastic shapes with the adhesive and stick it in the bottom right corner of the window.

5. Pick a shape in one of the other colors, lightly spray it with the adhesive, and fit it next to the first shape. Repeat this process row after row. Don't worry if the pieces overlap a bit. It will look amazing when it's all done, I promise.

6. When you've filled the entire window with full pieces, it's time to fill in the edges with partial pieces. Hold each piece up to the window and mark it lightly so you know where to cut.

7. Cut the edge pieces to fit, lightly spray them with the adhesive, and stick them to the window to complete the entire pattern.

SCRAP-FABRIC DOOR BEADS

I'm not going to lie to you: These took some time to make. But it was worth it! For ages my craft room was filled with small pieces of fabric that I didn't know what to do with. When I saw a row of little scrap-fabric birds on a recent trip to Mexico, this idea popped into my head. The best thing about these door beads is that, because of the fabric, they don't make noise every time you walk through them. So hunker down and get in touch with your inner hippie. *Peace out,* my brothas and sistas!

YOU'LL NEED:

5 yards of different pieces of scrap fabric

Scissors

Measuring tape

Sewing machine

Thread in any color

Wire hanger

Pliers

12 glass chips or marbles per strand (I used about 350 for this doorway)

Tension rod or nails to hang the strips

Hint: In case you don't know what bias is, pretend you have a perfect square of fabric. If you fold it in half to create a triangle, the length of the fold is the bias. When you cut fabric on the bias, it has stretch. Pretty cool, right?

HERE'S HOW:

1. Fold the fabrics so you can cut 3"-wide bias strips as shown.

2. Cut as many strips as possible—you're going to need a lot! Each strand of door beads will require a combined piece of fabric that's as long as your door opening plus 18". So if your door is 72" high, you'll need strands that are 90" long.

3. Stitch the pieces end to end on the sewing machine, using a straight stitch, to create about 25 long strips of combined fabric. If you're cutting the bias strips from large pieces of fabric, they'll already be quite long and it won't take much time to make the pieces you need.

4. When you're done sewing together the bias pieces, fold each strip in half lengthwise, with right sides together. Stitch the sides together, using a $\frac{1}{2}$" seam allowance, to make a long tube.

5. To turn the tubes right side out, first bend the wire hanger into a straight line and then bend a small hook on the wire's end with the pliers.

6. Slip the wire through each tube, hook it to the end by poking a small hole in the fabric, and pull the tube through itself.

7. Place a glass chip or marble in one end of the tube and make a knot on each side of it. Continue to do this every 8" or so—this part is really up to you.

8. When you're done, tie each strand to a tension rod placed in your door jamb. Or, since a rod may bend under the weight of the strands, you may want to hang them instead from small nails placed along the top of the jamb.

SPONGE-PAINTED CURTAIN PANEL

OK, I got a little carried away with the sponges, but if you like to print fabric as much as I do, this project should be a good inspiration. The thing I love about this pattern is that it would be wonderful on a porch or as a faux tile design on a wall in a plain bathroom. Now grab a sponge and get stampin'!

YOU'LL NEED:

2 cellulose sponges (medium size, about 3" x 5")

Scissors

Hot glue gun and glue stick

Small pieces of wood about 3" x 5"

Plain curtain panel

Newspaper or cardboard

Iron and ironing board (optional)

Flat paint in dark brown and mint green

Plastic plate

Scrap cardboard

Yardstick

HERE'S HOW:

1. Cut the four corners off one sponge to create a large tile-shaped stamp.

2. Cut a 1¼" square from the other sponge.

3. Hot glue the two sponge shapes onto small pieces of wood.

4. Lay the curtain panel out on newspaper or cardboard in a large workspace. Make sure it's nice and flat—iron it if you have to.

5. Pour a small amount of mint green paint onto a plastic plate.

6. Dip the large sponge stamp in the paint and practice printing on a piece of newspaper or cardboard to get the hang of it and to establish your design.

7. When you're confident, stamp the tile shape with the green paint all the way down one side of the curtain panel.

8. Make another row next to it, leaving a small blank space between the two rows.

9. Stamp two more rows the same way along the opposite edge of the curtain.

10. Stamp two more rows in the exact center of the curtain (as measured with the yardstick).

11. Stamp double rows between the other three sets, to make a total of five double rows altogether.

12. With the small stamp and the dark brown paint, stamp inside the diamond spaces between the green tile shapes, and inside the triangular spaces on each side of the double rows.

13. Once the paint is dry, hang the panel with curtain clips.

HAND-STITCHED CURTAIN PANEL

Talk about a major embroidery project! But this was so easy to do you wouldn't believe it. It was also really fun. I stitched large simple flowers and a bird, but you could create any sort of design—a huge cat or even your name!

YOU'LL NEED:

Iron and ironing board

Basic curtain panel

Pencil

Paper

Template on page 259 (optional)

Skeins of yarn

Large needle with an eye big enough for a piece of yarn

HERE'S HOW:

1. Iron your curtain panel.

2. Lay out the curtain on a large table so you can see most of it.

3. Sketch out your design first on a piece of paper. *Try this:* If your panel is 8' x 4', draw a rectangle 8" x 4" so you can see in miniature what your design will look like. If you want to include my bird as part of your design, use the template.

4. Lightly trace your design on the panel in pencil.

5. Thread a large needle with about 5 feet of yarn and tie a knot at the end.

6. Make 1½"-long stitches on the panel following the lines you've drawn.

7. Change the colors for different elements. I used yellow for the bird, white for the flowers.

8. Tie knots in the back to secure the yarn ends. Hang the curtain panel from clips for the best look.

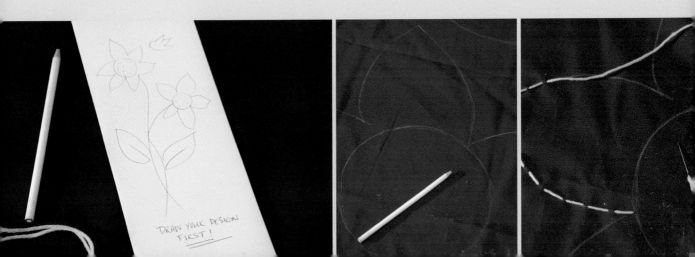

DRAW YOUR DESIGN FIRST !

ORGANZA-SQUARE CURTAIN

Windows are the eyes of the home, and everybody knows that great eyes deserve great shades. This textural drape doesn't take a high level of sewing skill, and you can jam to your favorite CD while you're making it. I'm pretty sure you won't have to iron this drape when you're done—how great is that! If you happen to have a little munchkin running around, he or she can hand you the squares as you go along. I have three who live next door, and do they come in handy when I have crafty projects to make!

YOU'LL NEED:

Basic drape panel (I got mine from Sure Fit)

Iron and ironing board (optional)

Pencil

Yardstick

3 yards of organza fabric

Scissors

Sewing machine and thread

HERE'S HOW:

1. If you've purchased a pre-made drape, as I did, don't bother ironing it before you start sewing; the creases on the folds will serve as great guides.

2. Once you've ironed (or unfolded) your drape, lay it flat and lightly pencil lines from top to bottom about 3" apart across the entire panel.

3. Make 3"-wide strips of the organza by snipping the selvage edge every 3" and ripping the fabric across to the other side.

4. Cut the strips into 3" squares with the scissors, and make a ton of them! For an average-size drape you'll need about 26 squares for each length you sew. (Divide the width of your drape, in inches, by 3 and multiply by 26 to figure out how many squares you'll need—and then make more, just in case).

5. Following the lines you've drawn on the panel, stitch on the organza squares one after another from the bottom of the drape to the top, arranging them so their corners are touching.

6. Repeat this process until the entire drape is covered. Hang the curtain with clips.

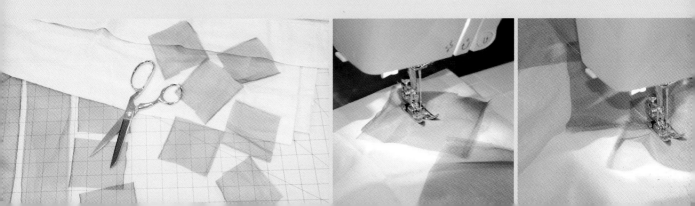

CHAPTER 5

AMAZING ACCENTS

This year I lost one of my favorite aunts, Ginny. She was awesome. Every candy bowl in her house was filled with something different and **she loved feeding us** from the time we walked in her front door to the time we left (a tradition I've carried on, as my big butt will attest!). **She collected everything** from ceramic clowns to tiny teapots; **her house was where all bric-a-brac went to retire.** I'm not kidding when I say she had thousands of figurines representing everything you can imagine. I remember her curly hair, her glasses, and her housedresses. She had a heart as big as Texas, and because of her I've always appreciated the little things in life. Aunt Ginny never forgot a birthday and expressed her love beautifully. She let us play with her collections and she made us feel at home even though her house was **quite like a little museum.**

When I make something to adorn my tabletops, I often think of her and how much **these accents make a difference in our homes.** They're **glittering expressions** of things that make us happy. Whether it be a decorative plate, a hand-carved box, an embellished frame, or a set of salt and pepper shakers in the shape of chickens, these things give us joy. **I say, down with minimalism—give me something to dust!**

MUST-HAVE MATTING

If you follow my work, you know I'll do anything with an old book page. I love printed words plastered all over everything from lamp bases to walls. I've had these antique postcards for years and didn't know how to make them look terrific until I thought of tossing them on top of some abstractly layered book scraps. It was cheap and easy to do, and I love the result! Why not print out some of your fun photos in black and white and do the same? This matting gives a great antique feel to any photo and would look amazing in a cluster of different-size frames.

YOU'LL NEED:

Picture frame (I think black looks best)

Book pages you can cut

Scissors

Elmer's Glue-All

Self-adhesive photo-mounting corners or ½"-wide strips of black paper

Old postcards or black-and-white photographs

Tape (double-sided if you have it)

HERE'S HOW:

1. Remove the cardboard that's provided with the frame. This is what you'll glue the book pages to.

2. Cut up some book pages in squares and at angles.

3. Glue them to the cardboard in all different directions until it's completely covered.

4. If you're using photo-mounting corners, place them on the page-covered cardboard in the position you'd like the photos or postcards to be mounted, and slip the images into the corners.

5. If you're using black paper instead, cut a 1"-long piece for each corner and wrap it around the front of the image, then tape the two ends to the back. Make loops of tape, attach them to the back of the pictures—or, if you have it, use double-sided tape—and stick the pictures on the cardboard.

6. Insert your arrangement in the frame and hang it on the wall.

FABULOUS FABRIC PLANT

I know what you're thinking: Why would anyone want a fabric plant? I have no idea! I just wanted one, so I made one. Isn't that what creativity is all about? Let's face it, you can find silk plants aplenty. But ones made with scraps, well, they're one of a kind! I may start inventing new plants, just to freak people out when they come to my house.

YOU'LL NEED:

Scissors

About 2 yards of fabric scraps

Sewing machine

Thread that matches the fabric

Rebar tie wire

Wire cutters

Block of Styrofoam

Planter box or pot

HERE'S HOW:

1. Cut about 40 long, thin fabric triangles in different sizes. Mine ranged from 8" to 20" long and were never more than 4" wide at the base.

2. Fold each triangle in half lengthwise and sew up to the tip using ¼" seam allowance. Make sure you leave enough room to slip the wire inside each triangle.

3. Cut rebar tie wire about 4" longer than the first "leaf."

4. Slip the wire inside the fabric, all the way to the tip.

5. Stick the excess wire at the other end into the Styrofoam base.

6. Continue this way with the remaining "leaves" until your plant comes to life. Nestle the Styrofoam base in a planter box or pot.

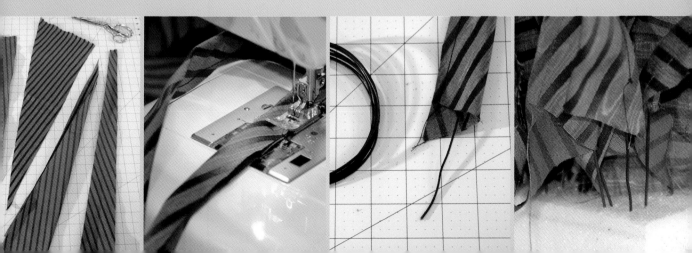

POPSICLE STICK PLANTER BOX

I don't care what anyone says—Popsicle sticks are craftastic and I will continue to use them until the day they lay me in my coffin (which, by the way, will be made from Popsicle sticks). I've never understood why people are so offended by them. Perhaps it brings them back to a not-so-successful craft project? Regardless, this planter is one of my favorite projects in the book because it was made completely from scratch. I absolutely love it and hope you do too.

YOU'LL NEED:

Four 11 ½"-long 1" x 12" pine boards

Hammer

Fifteen 1 ¾" finishing nails

Elmer's Wood Glue

One 12 ¾"-long 1" x 12" pine board

Drill with ¼" drill bit

500 Popsicle sticks

Band saw or heavy-duty scissors

Minwax Wood Stain (water-based) in a shade of blue

1"-wide paintbrush

Heavy-duty plastic bag

Scissors

Staple gun

HERE'S HOW:

1. Nail four 11 ½"-long boards together to make a box (use wood glue at the joints).

2. Nail the 12 ¾"-piece on the bottom.

3. Drill a hole in the bottom of the box to allow for drainage if you're using it for a plant.

4. Cut the Popsicle sticks in half with heavy-duty scissors or a band saw.

5. Glue the sticks on with the wood glue like shingles, starting from the bottom, working toward the top, and overlapping them. Make sure to stagger them so they look interesting!

6. When you've covered the box, brush on the stain according to the instructions on the can.

7. To protect the wood, line the box with a heavy-duty plastic bag (cut it if you need to), and use the staple gun to attach it.

8. Cut a hole in the plastic right above the hole you drilled in the bottom of the box so your plants can drain.

BUTTERFLIES UNDER GLASS

I love going to the Museum of Natural History in New York and looking at all the bugs and butterflies behind glass. OK, I'm a big fan of the woolly mammoths, too, but I couldn't figure out a way to put one of those under glass in my living room. Lately I've been buying a lot of those faux butterflies made from beautifully painted feathers. Check your local craft store for packages of them—they're hard to resist. You can create your own curio cabinet and impress your friends with your beautiful collection.

YOU'LL NEED:

2"- or 3"-square wood block

Drill with ¼" drill bit

Twig(s) from your yard

Hot glue gun and glue stick

Ruler

Scissors

Glass vase

1 or 2 packages of different-size faux butterflies

Glass candle plate (large enough to cover the mouth of the vase)

HERE'S HOW:

1. Drill a hole in the wood block large enough to fit the base of the twig(s).

2. Insert the twig(s) and hold in place with hot glue.

3. Measure the inside of the vase and cut the twig(s) to fit inside the vase when it's upside down.

4. Carefully glue the butterflies in place on the twig(s).

5. As you apply each butterfly, put the vase (upside down) over the twig(s) to make sure there's enough room inside.

6. When you're done gluing on all the butterflies, glue the wood base to the glass plate.

7. Cover the arrangement with the vase and glue the vase to the candle plate to keep it from shifting around.

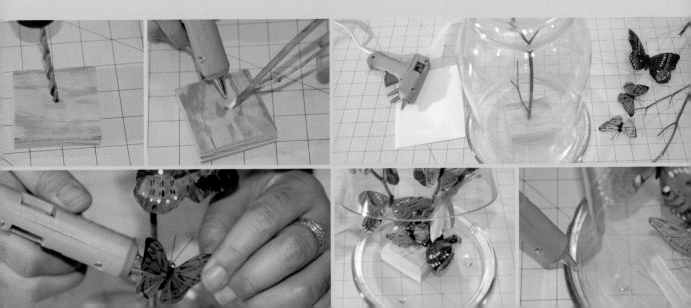

EAGLE LADY SCULPTURE

I've always been a fan of half-man/half-animal creatures. From centaurs to mermaids, I love them all. When I visited Donridge (Tony Duquette's home in Beverly Hills), I noticed that he had lions with women's heads guarding his front door. I immediately decided that I, too, had to have half-and-half creatures in my home to spark conversation. I hunted around and found some great garden sculptures at very decent prices. (Check out garden centers, flea markets, and street vendors.) This eagle sculpture was pretty boring until I did a Henry VIII and added a woman's head. OK, a bit morbid, but you get the point!

YOU'LL NEED:

2 plaster sculptures about the same size (so when you switch the heads, they look like they belong together)

Tape measure

Pencil

Jigsaw, hacksaw (which will take a bit longer), or Dremel tool

Rag

Amazing Goop Household glue

Masking tape

Tile grout (smooth, not latex grout—like a thick plaster)

Sandpaper

Paint to match your sculpture pieces (optional)

HERE'S HOW:

1. Measure around the neck of the two sculptures to find where their diameters are the closest. At that point, draw a line around the neck of each one.

2. Using a saw or Dremel tool, carefully cut off the head of each sculpture along the line you've drawn. Clean off the dust with a rag.

3. Glue the new head on the sculpture, and tape it in place so it doesn't move. It's fine if the positioning is a little off—don't worry. Just put the head in the position and prop it up with a wad of paper or whatever you need to keep it in place so the glue can adhere where you want it.

4. When the glue dries and the head is stable, remove the tape. Use some tile grout to fill in the cracks and spaces so the sculpture looks nice.

5. When the grout dries, sand around the neck to give it a finished look.

6. Paint it if you wish. Then plop it down right in the middle of your coffee table and watch how people react.

TRAMP ART CARDBOARD FRAME

I can't resist picking up shipping boxes at the post office because the cardboard they're made of is so easy to work with—you can even cut small pieces of it with scissors rather than a craft knife. It's great for projects from book binding to simple frames to really fun sets of postcards. These cardboard frames look much more complicated than they really are. Once you get the hang of it, you'll realize it's just cardboard and glue and some time. You can always experiment and make other frames, so have fun with it!

YOU'LL NEED:

Cardboard shipping boxes from the post office (they're free!)

Pencil

Craft knife

Scissors

Elmer's Glue-All

10" of ribbon for hanging

Hot glue gun and glue stick

HERE'S HOW:

1. Decide on your basic frame shape. My suggestion is to start with something simple and experiment as you learn the technique. Try a basic square frame that you will fill with other squares and triangles. Whatever frame shape you choose, cut it out from a large piece of cardboard using the craft knife.

2. Use the scissors to cut out a smaller shape you like—let's say a simple square—to adorn the frame.

3. Trace that first square for the second one, but this time cut it out a little smaller than the first.

4. Trace the second square and cut out a new one, making the third square a little smaller than the second. Getting the hang of it now?

5. Continue until you've made four or more of the concentric squares (or other shapes). Place them on top of each other and you'll see that they're forming a kind of pyramid.

6. Glue the pile of squares together with Elmer's and then glue the whole stack to your frame.

7. Repeat the process with the same shape, or other shapes, to fill the entire frame. As you pile them up, the frame will start to take on an interesting form.

8. Cut a large piece of cardboard for the back of the frame and attach your photo or artwork, again using Elmer's.

9. A simple ribbon hot glued to the back is a great way to hang the frame.

COLORIFIC TEA SET

Have you ever found a great but beat-up tea set that just made you sad? Barely any silver left, maybe a dent or two, and even a bent handle? Well, I did and it made me ecstatic! I had finally found the perfect tea set to paint any way I wanted. After spending just $5 for all three pieces at a junk sale, I'm now the envy of afternoon tea drinkers everywhere. Break out the cucumber sandwiches, folks, and let's party!

YOU'LL NEED:

An old silver tea set (or just a teapot)

Silver polish

Fine sandpaper

Rag

Rubbing alcohol

Masking tape

Newspapers

Krylon Fusion spray paint

Krylon Crystal Clear enamel spray coating (high gloss)

HERE'S HOW:

1. Clean your tea set with silver polish to get off all the tarnish.

2. Sand the pieces with fine sandpaper and then remove all the dust. Wipe down the pieces with rubbing alcohol.

3. Tape around the inside of the mouth of each piece so that spray paint doesn't get inside. Set the pieces on newspaper outdoors.

4. With small strokes, lightly spray paint each piece. *Important:* Take your time painting these pieces. Don't overspray them! Use several light coats of paint spaced about 10 minutes apart for the most professional look.

5. After the pieces are completely dry, spray them with protective finish. Use light coats, waiting 10 minutes between coats, until the pieces are glossy and beautiful. Let them dry for one week before use, allowing the paint to harden perfectly and keep the set from chipping when you use it. Hand wash with warm soapy water and a soft sponge.

DECORATIVE DRAWER KNOBS

I found these simple knobs at The Home Depot for very little money and thought they would be terrific for a project. Here are some ideas that might inspire you to change out your drawer knobs and spice up your furniture.

YOU'LL NEED:

Glass chips

Images the size of the glass chips

Pencil

Scissors

Elmer's Glue-All

1"-wide paintbrush

Amazing Goop Household glue

Basic flat drawer knobs

Large fabric flowers

Large gems (a bit smaller than the knob)

HERE'S HOW:

To make knobs with glass-chip images:

1. Place a glass chip on top of your image and trace around the chip.

2. Cut out the image just a bit smaller than the shape you've drawn.

3. Brush a thin layer of Elmer's on the image and adhere it to the back of the glass chip so you can see it from the front.

4. When it's dry, use a generous amount of Goop glue to attach the chip to the knob. You're done!

To make knobs with flowers:

Using Goop, glue fabric flowers on the knobs. OK, you're done!

To make knobs with gems:

Using Goop, glue gems on the knobs. OK, you're done!

REBAR WIRE DRAWER HANDLES

These are cool-looking, inexpensive drawer handles that you can make in a pinch. They'll work with just about any drawers that have holes drilled for traditional metal handles. Super simple to make, they use just one material: rebar tie wire. It's one of my favorite hardware store finds, and I use it for lots of home décor projects.

YOU'LL NEED:

Rebar tie wire

Wire cutters

Ruler

Pliers

HERE'S HOW:

1. Cut two pieces of wire about 3" longer than the distance between the screw holes for your handles.

2. Cut one piece of wire about 16" long.

3. Hold the three wires together evenly at one end. About 1½" up, start wrapping the two wires with the third long wire.

4. Continue wrapping until you're about 1½" from the other end.

5. Snip off any excess so all three wires are the same length.

6. Slip the three wires through the screw holes and bend with pliers to keep them in place.

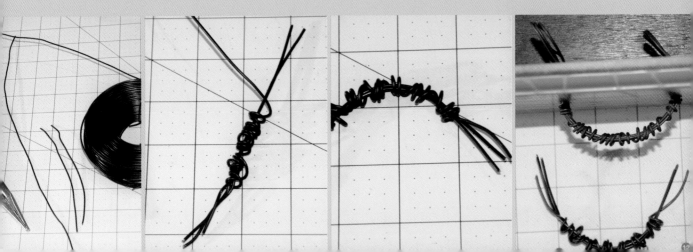

ROPE DRAWER PULL

Here's just another example of how you can spruce up a boring drawer knob. By the way, when I see an old dresser on the street ready for trash pick-up, I usually pull out my trusty screwdriver keychain and take off the knobs for later use. You'd be surprised by how many things you can do with old dresser knobs.

YOU'LL NEED:

Knob to decorate

10" of decorative rope per knob

Hot glue gun and glue stick

Amazing Goop Household glue

Transparent tape

HERE'S HOW:

1. Start at the center of the knob and hot glue the edge of the rope right in the middle.

2. Spiral the rope around and around and attach it using Goop glue until you reach the very edge of the knob.

3. Tuck the end of the rope under the knob where you can't see it and use hot glue to attach it.

4. Dab a bit of the Goop glue on the end as well so it will really stay in place.

5. Put some transparent tape over the whole knob to keep the rope in place until it dries. After about 10 minutes, remove the tape.

PLASTER MASK PLANTER

I love anything you can use as a mold. When I saw these Halloween masks, the first thing I thought of was casting them in plaster of Paris. Well, the results were terrific, turning my boring garden pots into something spectacular. My pots were cheapie plastic ones and I cut off some of the rim with scissors to get the mask to fit just right. Pots come in many different shapes and sizes, so take your mask to the store with you to figure out which will work best.

YOU'LL NEED:

Plaster of Paris

Container to mix plaster

Halloween mask that you can fill with plaster

Packing tape

Plastic or terra-cotta pot

Sandpaper or craft knife

Amazing Goop Household glue, or hot glue gun and glue stick

Tile adhesive caulk

Krylon Fusion spray paint in white

Gray paint

Paintbrush

HERE'S HOW:

1. Mix enough plaster of Paris to fill your mask. If your mask has holes in it for the eyes and mouth, tape over them on the outside of the mask, not on the inside where you'll be pouring the plaster.

2. Pour the plaster into the mask. Let the plaster dry, then remove the mask.

3. With sandpaper or a craft knife, scratch the pot and the back of the plaster face so the glue has something to hold on to.

4. Using Amazing Goop glue or hot glue, put the face on the planter and let it dry in place. Squeeze some tile adhesive caulk into the edges where the plaster face doesn't touch the side of the pot.

5. After the face has dried in place, fill the sides with more caulk. I did this to make it look more finished, but honestly it would look fine even without this step.

6. On newspaper outdoors, spray the pot white after the caulk has dried.

7. Using gray paint over the white, dry brush the pot. For this technique, dip the brush in paint and then remove as much of the paint as possible before applying it to the surface. That way it will streak and leave the under color showing through, making the features pop. Continue dry brushing until you achieve the look you want.

8. Fill the pot with a bushy plant and it will look like green hair!

BIRD-ON-A-BRANCH DINNER NAPKINS

No one loves a pretty dinner napkin more than I do, especially one that I made. These match my kitchen birdcage pillows on page 42. You might try this idea on a skirt or even a white cotton shirt just for kicks. Edging a tablecloth could be fun, too. You could make napkins with wonderful designs that say, "If you get food on me you'll never be invited to dinner again!" Let your imagination fly.

YOU'LL NEED:

Template on page 258

Paper

Pencil

Scissors

12"-square sheet of contact paper

Craft knife

Plain cloth dinner napkin

Hole punch

Newspaper

Krylon Fusion spray paint

Sewing machine with zigzag stitch

Thread

HERE'S HOW:

1. Trace a bird template onto paper, cut it out, and trace it onto contact paper.

2. Cut out the bird with a craft knife and stick the relief (the part with the bird hole in it!) onto the napkin where you want it.

3. Use the hole punch to make a dot for the bird's eye out of contact paper and stick it in place. Place the napkin on newspaper outdoors.

4. Cover the rest of the napkin with newspaper so that only the bird part gets sprayed with paint.

5. Lightly spray the bird three times, waiting about 8 minutes between coats.

6. When the paint is completely dry, lightly sketch out the branches.

7. On your sewing machine zigzag over the branches you've sketched. Now it's time to invite people to dinner—but only if they're very neat eaters!

CORK STAMPS

There are all kinds of ways to make stamps—from potatoes (not my favorite!) to the sticky foam that kids use. Lately I've been using cork just for fun. It reminds me of the wooden stamps that were used in early printing presses. I've created several different designs here, but trust me: The patterns you can come up with are endless. I encourage you to experiment on pieces of fabric and paper before you begin so you can get the feel of the stamping. After that, try it on things like a plain white blouse that has a stain or on your dingy white pillowcases to give them new life.

YOU'LL NEED:

Image or design of your choice

Thin sheets of cork (it's sold in rolls or squares)

Pen or pencil

Craft knife

E-6000 glue

Small blocks of wood in different sizes

Paint

Shallow container for the paint or 1"-wide paintbrush

HERE'S HOW:

1. First you have to find some designs that you like. In this book I've used flowers, leaves, and traditional Suzani designs—feel free to copy mine if you can't find any you like. Once you get going, you won't run out of ideas; but if you do, you can always hop on the Internet and look around for inspiration.

2. Draw or trace your design onto the cork and carefully cut it out with a craft knife on a cutting mat.

3. Glue the cork pieces to the wood block and let them dry for a few hours.

4. When you're ready to print, pour a small puddle of paint into the container and dip your stamp in it. For a cleaner image, use a paintbrush to apply the color to the stamp. Either way, once the paint is on the stamp, print away!

5. Dip the stamp again or reapply paint with the brush as needed.

CLEAR PLASTIC BOX FRAME WALL CLOCK

My friend Peter has a huge clock in his kitchen that he made from a large plastic frame and a large collage of friends and family. I love it! He agreed to let me use his idea for this book. My version is a bit different from his, but I would never have come up with it if it weren't for the vision of my lovely friend.

YOU'LL NEED:

Image enlarged to 18" x 24"

18" x 24" plastic box frame

Drill and ⅜" drill bit

Contact paper

Scissors

Newspaper

Krylon Fusion spray paint in fluorescent orange

Craft knife

Cardboard cut to the size of the box frame

Elmer's Craft Bond Spray Adhesive

Clock that you can take apart (check the 99¢ store)

Clear packing tape

HERE'S HOW:

1. Choose a suitable image. Mine is from a Dover book with mortised advertising images that are perfect for clocks.

2. Place your image inside the frame and decide where you want the clock parts to be placed.

3. Drill a hole in the frame for your clock parts.

4. With the image inside the frame, cut an oval out of contact paper to use as a stencil for the fluorescent paint. I cut out leaves and clovers and added them to the oval so it would have more interest. I placed one in the lower right corner and in other random spots.

5. Peel the backing from the contact paper and stick the oval and other flourishes to the outside of the frame. Place it on newspaper outdoors.

6. Spray paint the frame with the fluorescent paint and let it dry for 5 minutes. Then carefully remove the contact paper. If you're having a hard time getting it off, use the tip of a craft knife to lift an edge.

7. Place the cardboard inset inside the frame and cut out a hole where your clock parts will fit. My clock was square, so I traced it and cut out the exact size.

8. Spray adhesive on the image, adhere it to the cardboard inset, and put it inside the box frame.

9. Poke a hole from the inside of the frame outward through the hole you drilled.

10. Remove the clock hands and push the shaft (where the clock hands were attached) through the hole.

11. Tape the clock in place with packing tape.

12. Replace the clock hands and you're done—just in time.

YARN-WRAPPED TWIG ARRANGEMENT

This project took some time, but I found it quite relaxing. Now I'm thinking about making branches using all different kinds of yarn, from fuzzy to metallic. You can make a beautiful, unique arrangement for the cost of a skein of yarn and a little bit of time.
If you don't want to put twigs in a vase, make a large branch and hang it on the wall. Either way, you'll find that these arrangements will enhance any room.

YOU'LL NEED:

1 skein of yarn

Yardstick

Scissors

Twigs or small branches

Hot glue gun and glue sticks

HERE'S HOW:

1. Cut a length of yarn about 6' long.

2. Tie a knot with the yarn around the base of one branch and start wrapping upward.

3. When you have about 10" of yarn left, tie another 6'-long piece of yarn to it and continue to wrap until the entire branch is covered.

4. Dot some hot glue to keep the end in place when you've reached the tip of the branch.

5. Repeat this process with several other branches until you've created an amazing arrangement.

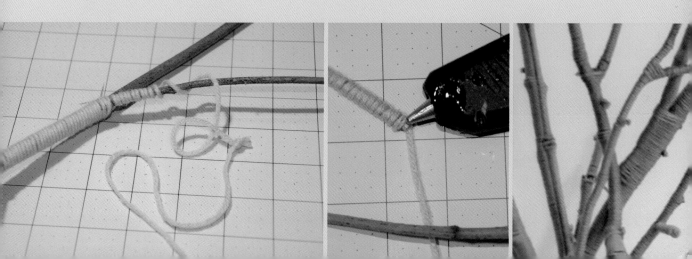

PLASTER-DIPPED FLOWER FRAME AND LAMP

In many a grandmother's house you could find objects with tiny porcelain flowers on them—delicate pastel flowers jutting out from little vases or frames. I was so in love with those beautiful little flowers, and for years I've been trying to make something even remotely similar. My first few attempts were a disaster. Let's just say a lot of faux flowers found their way to the garbage can before I finally figured out a great process. Here's what I came up with.

YOU'LL NEED:

Newspaper

Aluminum foil

Faux fabric flowers

Plaster of Paris

Container to mix the plaster in

Rubber gloves (optional)

Elmer's Glue-All

1"-wide paintbrush

Basic frame or lamp base to decorate

Amazing Goop Household glue

Krylon Fusion spray paint in black (flat)

Latex paint in metallic gold

HERE'S HOW:

1. Spread out some newspaper and aluminum foil.

2. Pull the faux flowers from their stems.

3. Mix up a batch of plaster.

4. Put on rubber gloves if you like. Dip the flowers in the plaster, making sure to cover the entire flower, and place them on the foil to dry.

5. Make as many flowers as you'll need to cover your frame or lamp base (or both). I used about 18 flowers and 10 leaves in different sizes for my frame. For the lamp base I used about 10 flowers and 15 leaves. It all depends on how much you want to put on your items.

6. Once the flowers are dry, cover them in Elmer's glue using the paintbrush—really soak them. Put them back on the foil to dry.

7. When the flowers are dry, peel them off the foil and arrange them on the frame or lamp base.

8. Glue them on with a generous amount of Goop glue.

9. When the flowers have dried in place, put the whole frame or lamp base on newspaper outdoors. Spray paint the entire object with the black paint, and let dry for 20 minutes.

10. With a small paintbrush, go over the edges with metallic gold paint to give the flowers some definition.

CHAPTER 6

CAPTIVATING CANDLELIGHT

Have you ever noticed how wonderful everyone looks by candlelight? Look around any romantic, candlelit restaurant and you'll see how attractive all the people are. They **exchange flirty glances** across the table, twist their hair between their fingertips, and **move their eyebrows in all sorts of directions.** How they look in the parking lot a few minutes later is a different story for quite a few of these folks, so I always hope they clinch the deal during dinner! But let me get back to what I was saying. **Candles can create romance and mood.** They give that soft glow to the world that we need sometimes when the harsh glare of reality is just too much. I like to think of a time when all the lighting in the world was candlelight. **Every once in a while I have an evening of no noise, just candles and thought and a bowl of Fiddle Faddle.** It's a great way to hear myself think and take a break from the constant input of information—music, television shows, magazines—that occupies me most of the time. The silver tray sconces in this chapter are a throwback to an era before electricity and even gas lighting. **My favorite candle** apparatus here is the 99¢ store ceramic birdhouse candelabra. It's just plain fun, and I had a blast making it.

SILVER TRAY WALL SCONCE

You should grab silver trays whenever you see them at thrift stores or yard sales because they have so many uses. Even a little banged up, they can be really chic on a party table. Hey, you can't see the scratches through all the cheese and crackers anyway! I turned my trays into wall sconces that beautifully reflect the light when the candles are lit.

YOU'LL NEED:

Silver or metal tray

Silver polish

Flat, bendable decorative hook

Sandpaper

Pliers

Template on page 259

Paper

Fine-point permanent marker

Scissors

1 sheet of 4" x 6" aluminum flashing

Heavy-duty scissors or tin shears

E-6000 glue

Small-gauge wire

HERE'S HOW:

1. Clean the tray with polish, removing the tarnish and grime.

2. Sand the back of the hook. Bend the hook to a 90-degree angle.

3. Trace the template onto paper with the marker, cut out the shape, then trace it onto the flashing.

4. Cut out the shape from the flashing and bend up the sides (this is where you'll place your candle).

5. Glue the shaped flashing to the bent-out part of the hook.

6. Using a generous amount of glue, attach the back of the hook to the tray, toward the bottom, and let the glue dry.

7. Stretch a piece of wire across the back of the tray, toward the top. Make a little spiral of wire on each end, and glue the ends to the back of the tray for hanging.

8. When the glue is dry, hang the sconce, add a candle, and see the light!

CERAMIC BIRDHOUSE CANDELABRA

I'd been seeing these cute little ceramic birdhouses everywhere and decided to pick up a few and keep them around just to see what I could come up with. When I found some wire branch jewelry holders, I thought, I'll make a candelabra! I think it looks really cool all painted in black but it would look just as cool entirely covered in glitter. I can't wait until the candelabra is covered with drips of wax and looks 100 years old.

YOU'LL NEED:

2 or 3 wire structures
(try the 99¢ store)

Amazing Goop Household glue

12" x 14" wood scrap

Pencil

Jigsaw (optional)

Template on page 259

Paper

Scissors

Fine-point permanent marker

12"-square sheet of aluminum flashing

Tin shears or heavy-duty scissors

Pliers

Transparent tape

5 small ceramic birdhouses

Newspaper

Krylon Fusion spray paint in black

HERE'S HOW:

1. Glue the wire structures together so they will support your houses. Bend them if you need to.

2. Place the glued-together structure on top of the scrap wood. If you don't have a jigsaw, just use the square piece of wood for the base.

3. If you do have a jigsaw, trace a line on the wood base around the wire structure, then cut out the shape with the jigsaw.

4. Glue the wire structure to the base.

5. While the base is drying, trace the birdhouse chimney template onto paper, cut it out, then trace as many chimneys as there are birdhouses onto the aluminum flashing. Use shears or heavy-duty scissors to cut out the chimneys and bend them into shape.

6. Glue the chimneys onto the birdhouses and tape them in place to dry.

7. When the base is dry, glue the birdhouses onto the wire structure. Use plenty of glue—it will be covered in paint, so you won't see it! Bend the wire as needed to keep the birdhouses in place and the candelabra stable.

8. Once everything is dry, remove the tape and put the candelabra on newspaper outdoors. Spray paint the entire piece black. Use several coats, waiting about 10 minutes between coats.

9. Set small candles in the chimneys.

MIRRORED GLASS CANDLEHOLDERS

I have been coveting candleholders like these for years, but the true antique ones are way out of my price range. Fortunately, I've figured out how to make my own version for very little money, and now I can have as many as I want. Just don't tell anyone my secret, OK? Simply head to the thrift store for different-size vases, large dessert dishes, and other such pieces; even clear light fixtures will work. Super easy to make, these candleholders are also beautiful. Several clustered together make an amazing table centerpiece.

YOU'LL NEED:

Various glass pieces

Newspaper

Krylon Looking Glass spray paint

Amazing Goop Household glue

Masking tape

Sticky felt for the bottom

Pencil

Scissors

HERE'S HOW:

1. Experiment with the different glass pieces. Groups of 2 and 3 work best for these candleholders. Stack them to see how they will look glued together.

2. Lay the pieces on newspaper outdoors. Spray the inside of each with the paint until you get the desired reflective quality.

3. When the paint is dry, glue the pieces together. Use masking tape to keep them from shifting as they dry.

4. Trace the shape of each bottom piece of glass onto the backing of the sticky felt. Cut the felt pieces, remove the backing, and adhere them to the candleholders.

5. Fill with candles and enjoy.

CAST-PLASTER PLANTER CANDLEHOLDER

Say that three times fast! Do you realize how many cool things you have around your house that would make terrific molds for plaster? Think about it for a moment: Halloween masks, funky dishes, plastic planters, old toys, doll heads. . . . If you can fill it with plaster, chances are it will result in something pretty cool. These candleholders have a great architectural feel to them, kind of like they were salvaged from an old building and found in a pile of bricks. In fact, it was on a quick trip to the 99¢ store that I found these fantastic molds. Now start digging through your stuff and let's get casting!

YOU'LL NEED:

Plaster of Paris

Plastic planter

Small glass votive holders
(I used 4 for the long project)

Cooking spray

Container to mix plaster in

Sandpaper

Latex paint in off-white

Paintbrush

Gold latex paint

Rags

Sticky felt (for the bottom)

Scissors

HERE'S HOW:

1. Determine how much plaster you'll need for your mold. A 10-pound bag will serve you well for several craft projects, and it's more economical to buy it in bulk than in smaller amounts.

2. Spray the planter on the inside and the glass votive holders on the outside with the cooking spray. This will help the plaster slip out easily once it's dry.

3. Mix the plaster in a large container and pour it into the planter.

4. Tap the planter with a spoon on the sides or tap it on a table to get out all the bubbles.

5. While the plaster is still wet, set the glass votive holders about 1" down in the plaster. Leave them there until the plaster has dried.

6. When the plaster is dry, twist out the votive holders, turn the planter upside down, and tap out the plaster cast. Let the cast dry at least another hour before you paint.

7. When the candleholder is completely dry, sand it to remove the rough edges.

8. Paint the whole thing with the off-white paint.

9. When the paint is dry, put some gold paint on a rag and rub the edges of the plaster to give it an antique look. If you get too much gold on it, go over it again with the white paint until you've achieved the desired effect.

10. Cut a piece of sticky felt for each side of the bottom and stick it on. Fill the candleholder with votive candles, place it on your table, and admire your beautiful centerpiece.

HANGING WIRE AND GLASS VOTIVE HOLDER

Hanging candles can make any outdoor space feel magical. Keep an eye out for unique glassware at thrift stores and yard sales, where it's almost always inexpensive. When combined with wire and filled with a candle, even the most mundane glass container can look amazing.

YOU'LL NEED:

Rebar tie wire

Yardstick

Wire cutters

Needle-nose pliers

Glass container

Chandelier drop (optional)

HERE'S HOW:

1. Cut two pieces of 25"-long rebar tie wire.

2. With the pliers, bend the pieces in a wiggly zigzag pattern and wrap them around the base and center of your glass.

3. Clip off the excess and twist the ends together as you would a twist tie, or make interlocking loops and tighten them with pliers.

4. If you need to make the wire tighter, just squeeze the zigzags closer together.

5. Decide how long you want your candleholder to hang. I like it to be about 30".

6. Cut two wires, one about 33" long and the other about 66" long.

7. Bend the middle of the 66" wire to fit across the bottom of the glass, then thread each end through the bottom and top zigzags.

8. Loop the very end of the 33" wire around the 66" wire at the bottom of the glass and thread it up through the zigzags.

9. If you wish, you can now attach a chandelier drop to the wire at the bottom of the glass.

10. Wrap the tops of the three long wires together, make a loop, and hang the holder from a hook.

11. Drop in a candle, and you've got some terrific mood lighting.

CHAPTER 7

TERRIFIC TABLES

Tables really are terrific. **I'm sitting here at a coffee shop writing at a perfect little table.** And after a really strong margarita, I'm often under a table wondering why I can't hold my liquor! Think about it: Without tables, the Last Supper would have been known as the Last Picnic, and we would never be able to table a discussion again. Even worse, **where would we put our big coffee table books?** We just can't do a darn thing without tables—and they are **crucial** to how we live our lives. I, for one, do not take them for granted and neither should you.

The **most fantastic table in the entire world** (and I mean entire world here!) is **the IKEA Parsons table** (called Lack), which retails for less than $15. You see them everywhere, even in the most expensive homes, and **they come in every color under the sun.** I love to use them as a place to nail and paste anything that will stick to them. I've been known to buy 5 or 6 at a time and keep them in my house until I decide what to do with them. If, by chance, you're not a fan of this table, that's fine. Check out your local thrift store for the unwanted tables that need **your special brand of creativity.** They are there, they are **abundant**, and they are **waiting for you** to take them home and make them **a special part of your life.** After all, you can't live without them, no matter how hard you try.

CHINESE MAT—COVERED TABLE

OK, raise your hand if there's a table in your house that you can't look at for another minute. Every time you walk by, it just stares at you and says, "I'm ugly, but you're afraid to get rid of me!" And then it says something else: "You don't have the nerve to get rid of me—where would you pile up your junk mail?!" Well, it's time to shut up that annoying table once and for all and give it a face-lift. It will make you happy, and the only thing your table will say when you pass by will be "thank you."

YOU'LL NEED:

Square or rectangular table

Measuring tape

2 woven Chinese mats

Scissors

Elmer's Wood Glue

2"-wide soft bristle brush

Hot glue gun and glue sticks

1 roll of ⅜" grosgrain ribbon that matches the mats (I used olive green)

Minwax Polycrylic Protective Finish

HERE'S HOW:

1. Measure your tabletop and cut one of the mats to that size.

2. Spread wood glue all over the tabletop with the brush and apply the mat. Use a nice amount of glue, as the mat has to be permanently attached. Let the glue dry.

3. Measure the table legs and cut the other mat in pieces to wrap around the legs.

4. Brush wood glue generously on the legs and adhere the mat pieces.

5. When the entire table is covered, use the hot glue gun to attach the grosgrain ribbon around all the edges. Take your time, and make sure you're covering all the rough edges of the mat with the ribbon.

6. Coat the entire table (even the ribbon!) with the Polycrylic and let it dry.

MOROCCAN SIDE TABLE

Every room needs a bright beautiful table to catch the eye. This one was super easy to make and I know your version will outshine mine. Ask the local lumber yard to cut the wood to size for you, as I did.

YOU'LL NEED:

Template on page 260

Four 22"-long pieces of 1" x 12" pine

Jigsaw

Sandpaper or electric sander

Two 18 ½"-long pieces of 1" x 10" pine

Elmer's Wood Glue

1 box of 2" finishing nails

Hammer

Newspaper

Krylon Fusion spray paint in blue

6 yards each of several matching trims (try cord and plastic beads)

Hot glue gun and glue stick

Buttons (optional)

HERE'S HOW:

1. Following the template, cut out the shape from the 22" pieces of wood and smooth with sandpaper or an electric sander.

2. Cut the corners off one long side of each 18 ½" piece of wood at a 45-degree angle, starting and ending 4" away from each corner. Sand to remove any rough edges.

3. Attach the four 22" sides together to create the base, applying a long line of wood glue and then nailing the pieces in place.

4. Put the two 18 ½" pieces together on the table base and, using wood glue and nails, attach them to the base.

5. Sand off any dirt or rough edges.

6. Lay the table on newspaper outdoors and spray paint it blue.

7. Apply several coats of paint, waiting at least 10 minutes between coats. Get the inside, too!

8. Using the glue gun, add trim around the edges of the table and around the design cutouts on the base. Take your time!

9. Glue old buttons around the tabletop to add a little something more, if you desire.

CHOPSTICK TABLE

Ever since they started selling chopsticks in huge bundles at the 99¢ store, I've been buying them up like they were going out of style. I'll eat anything with chopsticks—even spaghetti. Chopsticks remind me of Popsicle sticks, and you know how much I love to make projects out of those. This side table would look great with a piece of glass on top. Now let's get started—chop chop!

YOU'LL NEED:

600 chopsticks

Krylon Fusion spray paint in 5 different colors

Cardboard or newspaper

IKEA Lack table

Sandpaper

Elmer's Wood Glue

1"-wide paintbrush

Minwax Polycrylic Protective Finish

2"-wide paintbrush

HERE'S HOW:

1. Divide the chopsticks into five equal piles (120 each).

2. Spread one pile evenly across a piece of cardboard outdoors.

3. Spray the chopsticks with one color of paint and let them dry.

4. Do the same with the other four piles of chopsticks, each in a different color.

5. Sand the table so it has some texture. This will help the glue hold better.

6. Put the table on its side. Starting with the legs, glue on the chopsticks side by side, color side up, and work your way up to the tabletop. (The raw sides of the chopsticks get the glue.)

7. When you get near the tabletop, go a little crazy with the sticks and make the area look like a game of pickup sticks. *But make sure not to go above the rim of the table!*

8. Let the glue set for a while.

9. When you've completed one side and it's dry, flip the table and work on another side. Each side needs to dry well before you start on the next, so give yourself plenty of time.

10. Once all the sides are dry, flip the table upright and work on the tabletop. Starting in the center of the table, glue the chopsticks side by side in a row.

11. After the center row is finished, glue the rows on each side, then let them all dry.

12. Add more chopsticks in places that might have a little table peeking through. The more chopsticks you add, the more the table will look like it's made only of chopsticks.

13. Brush on the Polycrylic and let it dry.

FORNASETTI-ESQUE TABLE

I've done it. I've found a way to make metallic images adhere to furniture. This project isn't just about making a decoupage table, folks, it's about finding new ways to do it! My first failed attempt was to cover copy paper with gold spray paint and run it through a copy machine. Boy, did I get in trouble for that one! My next few attempts were just as unsuccessful. Then one day I realized that you could copy images onto clear acetate paper. The lightbulb went off, and so did I!

YOU'LL NEED:

Table in need of an overhaul

Newspaper

Krylon Fusion spray paint in black (high gloss)

Images to adhere

Copy center that makes acetate copies

Krylon Fusion spray paint in metallic gold

Scissors

Elmer's Glue-All

1"-wide paintbrush

Minwax Polycrylic Protective Finish (high gloss)

2"-wide paintbrush

Elmer's Painters pen in gold

HERE'S HOW:

1. Working on newspaper outdoors, spray paint your table with the black paint.

2. Copy your images at the copy center onto clear acetate paper.

3. Paint the back of the acetate with gold spray paint (the printing is on the front).

4. Once the metallic paint is dry, cut out the images from the acetate.

5. Experiment with the images, moving them around the table to figure out where they look best.

6. Using the 1" brush, paint the metallic side of the first image with glue and adhere it to the table.

7. Continue this process until the entire table is covered the way you want it.

8. After the images dry for a few hours, use the 2" brush to cover the entire table with the Polycrylic.

9. When the Polycrylic has dried, go around the table's edge with the gold pen to add a finishing touch.

Cut out
this shape
with
jigsaw
sand edges.

Wood Glue

GARDEN SIDE TABLE

I notice flowers in every aspect of design, whether they're rendered literally or translated abstractly. My belief is that flowers are to the earth what good accessories are to a home—absolutely essential for pulling it all together. Clustered together, these tables might even eliminate the need for fresh flowers in your home!

YOU'LL NEED:

Flower illustration or photo enlarged to 24"-square on 24 lb. paper (thinner paper will not work!)

Scissors

Transparent tape

Pen

24" x 24" piece of ½"-thick plywood

Jigsaw

Sandpaper

Elmer's Spray Adhesive

Two ½"-diameter plumber's flanges

Eight ½" wood screws

Drill with a Phillips head bit

One 11"-long piece of 1" x 12" pine plank

One 6"-long piece of 1" x 6" pine plank

One 24"-long piece of ½"-diameter plumber's pipe

Newspaper

Krylon Fusion spray paint in green

Elmer's Wood Glue

Minwax Polycrylic Protective Finish (high gloss)

1"-wide paintbrush

HERE'S HOW:

1. Cut out your flower image. Since this is a large image, you'll have several pieces to put together.

2. Tape the pieces together so you can see the exact size and shape of the flower.

3. Trace out the flower on top of the plywood.

4. With the jigsaw, carefully cut out the flower shape.

5. Sand the edges so your wood is smooth.

6. Using the spray adhesive, apply the flower image to the cut piece of wood.

7. With the drill, screw one of the flanges to the exact center of the back of the 11" piece of 1" x 12" plank.

8. Screw the other flange to the center of the back of the 6" piece of 1" x 6" plank.

9. Screw one end of the 24" piece of pipe to each flange, and make sure you screw it in tightly. This is your table base.

10. On newspaper outdoors, spray paint the base green to resemble a flower stem.

11. With wood glue, attach the bottom of the flower-shaped piece onto the 1" by 6" piece of pine and let it dry.

12. Once the glue is dry and the pieces are firmly in place, coat the tabletop with Polycrylic.

13. Let the tabletop dry—then start working on another one!

Hint: For any projects that call for glued or decoupaged images, make sure they're printed on paper that's at least 24 lbs. Thinner paper just won't work.

GLASS-TOP TABLE

You're looking at this and thinking, this guy is out of his mind! Well, though that may be true, you're going to love this project. You've seen those coffee tables with the horrible tops at the thrift store. You know the ones—they have cigarette burns on the top, and the wood is in terrible condition. Well, take a look under that table and check out the base. Chances are it's in pretty good condition and only needs a new top. If you can get a table with a decent glass top and a decent base, you're in luck. But if your great find doesn't have a glass top, check out the other ugly coffee tables at the thrift store or just head over to your local glass cutter and have one made to size. Pier 1 also sells glass tabletops in different sizes. I got this coffee table for $5 and the glass for another $15. I'd say a $20 coffee table is pretty darn good!

YOU'LL NEED:

Thrift store coffee table with great legs attached to a base

Screwdriver

Sandpaper

Rags

Newspaper

Krylon Fusion spray paint (high gloss) (I used Red Pepper)

Gold paint pen (Elmer's Painters pens work beautifully)

Plastic furniture no-slip dots

Glass top

HERE'S HOW:

1. Using your screwdriver, remove the tabletop from the base.
2. Sand the table base to get it in great shape for painting.
3. Dust off the base with rags.
4. On newspaper outdoors, spray the base with several coats of paint, waiting about 10 minutes between coats.
5. When the paint is dry, go along the edges with the gold pen to create accents.
6. Stick the plastic dots along the top of the table base, where the glass will be resting.
7. Place the glass on top and pile on the books and bric-a-brac!

CHAPTER 8

LUSCIOUS LIGHTING AND LAVISH LAMPSHADES

I don't like overhead lighting. No one looks good in it and it's never quite right. Trust me on this: If you want that weird spot on your head to show up, just switch on the overhead light. If not, take something—anything—and put a lightbulb in it to **create a fantastic lamp.** My two favorite places to find lamp inspiration are the 99¢ store and under the kitchen sink. **If I can find a way to glue it together and hang it from something with a lightbulb, I'm all over it!** I'm warning you, though, before you even start this chapter, to **use low-wattage bulbs** unless you're married to an electrician (who loves you). Better safe than sorry when it comes to making light fixtures. I'd have to say **my favorite light** in this chapter is the wire Calder-esque Butterfly Lamp. **I made the butterflies out of a 2-liter plastic bottle** and then spray painted them. Like I said, **if it's under my sink, it ends up on a lamp.** I hope this chapter "turns you on."

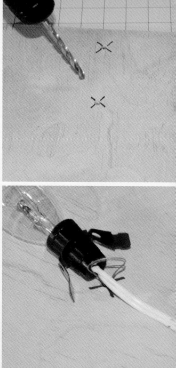
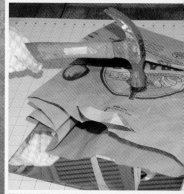

EXPLODING MIRROR SCONCE

I really think broken mirrors are beautiful, so they're anything but seven years of bad luck for me. When I turn on this mirror sconce at night, it's like a universe of stars reflected all over my home. Look for large discarded (preferably cracked) mirrors on the street on trash-collection day.

YOU'LL NEED:

8" x 10" piece of board

Drill with ⅜" drill bit

1' small-gauge wire

6' snap-in socket-and-cord set, with a switch on the cord and a candelabra base

Gloves

Goggles

Paper grocery bag

Hammer

Broken mirror pieces

Dremel tool with sanding bit

E-6000 glue

15-watt chandelier bulb

Safety Note: Always wear goggles that cover the entire eye area (not safety glasses) when you're working with glass or mirror pieces.

HERE'S HOW:

1. Prepare the base by drilling a hole in the center of the 8" x 10" board and another in the center toward the top that will later be used for hanging the sconce.

2. Wire the socket in place by sticking the small-gauge wire through the center hole from the back, wrapping it around the cord and securing it in place.

3. Put on your gloves and goggles, place the mirror in a paper bag, and smash with a hammer or heavy object to get small pieces (anywhere from 1" to 3" long). If you get larger pieces, just whack them one more time to make them smaller.

4. While still wearing your gloves and goggles, use the Dremel to sand the edges of each piece of mirror. I assure you this goes very quickly and you'll get the hang of it right away.

5. When you have a decent number of sanded pieces, glue them to the board, working slowly from the outside edge to the inside. It's great if the pieces stick up in some places and go in different directions—that will provide the best reflections.

6. When you get to the center where the bulb is, put a little glue on the socket to keep it in place. Then glue mirror pieces to the socket, making sure they won't get in the way of the lightbulb being screwed in.

7. Leave to dry for about 6 hours.

8. Place the sconce on a nail on the wall, put in the lightbulb, and plug it in to see if there are any bare spots or places where the shards of mirror should be sticking out more. Unplug the light and remove the bulb, add mirror pieces as needed, and let dry.

9. Replace the lightbulb and let it shine.

LAMINATED WALL SCONCE

I've always loved wallpaper and I'm always trying to find something to do with the wallpaper books left over from the local paint store. You see, I'm the guy who's always in there bugging them for the books as soon as they go out of season. Some of my favorite prints are of Chinese porcelain, and that's what I used for this laminated wall sconce. If you don't have large pieces of wallpaper, head over to Staples and have them enlarge a print that you can then tape together. You can make the sconce any size you want—my project was 17" x 36". It did take some patience and some fudging, but it was much easier than you might think. Besides, all my screaming and stress were worth it, since now you don't have to go through it.

YOU'LL NEED:

17" x 36" piece of wallpaper or enlarged image

Lamination machine (try Staples)

Scissors

Fine-point permanent marker

Ruler

10" x 12" piece of ½"-thick plywood

Drill with ¼" drill bit

40" of metal strapping

Tin shears or heavy-duty scissors

Eight ½" wood screws

Screwdriver

Craft knife

Transparent tape

Hammer and nail for hanging (optional)

Bread tie or small piece of wire

6' snap-in socket-and-cord set, with a switch on the cord and a candelabra base

15-watt chandelier bulb

HERE'S HOW:

1. Laminate your image. Cut off the excess lamination so the image is exactly 17" x 36", then put the image aside.

2. Mark a dot on the plywood in the center of the short side, 1" from the edge. Drill a hole at the mark. This is the hole you will use to hang the sconce on a nail.

3. Drill another hole about 3" down from the first one. This is the hole that will help you attach the socket for the lightbulb.

4. Cut the metal strapping into two 20"-long pieces. Mark a line 1 ½" from both ends of each piece and bend the metal there to a 90-degree angle.

5. With the screws and screwdriver, attach the 1 ½" part of one piece of metal to the back of the wood, at the very top. Curve the metal nicely across the front of the wood and attach it to the opposite side of the back. Do the same with the second piece of metal, this time attaching it toward the bottom of the wood piece.

6. On the back of the laminated image, use the marker and ruler to draw a grid of lines 1" apart from top to bottom and 4" apart from side to side.

7. With scissors or a craft knife, cut the image into pieces along the grid lines. *Warning:* Do not mix up the pieces! Keep them in the exact order in which you've cut them or you will drive yourself crazy! It's best to do this on a large table so you can keep track of everything.

Instructions continue on next two pages.

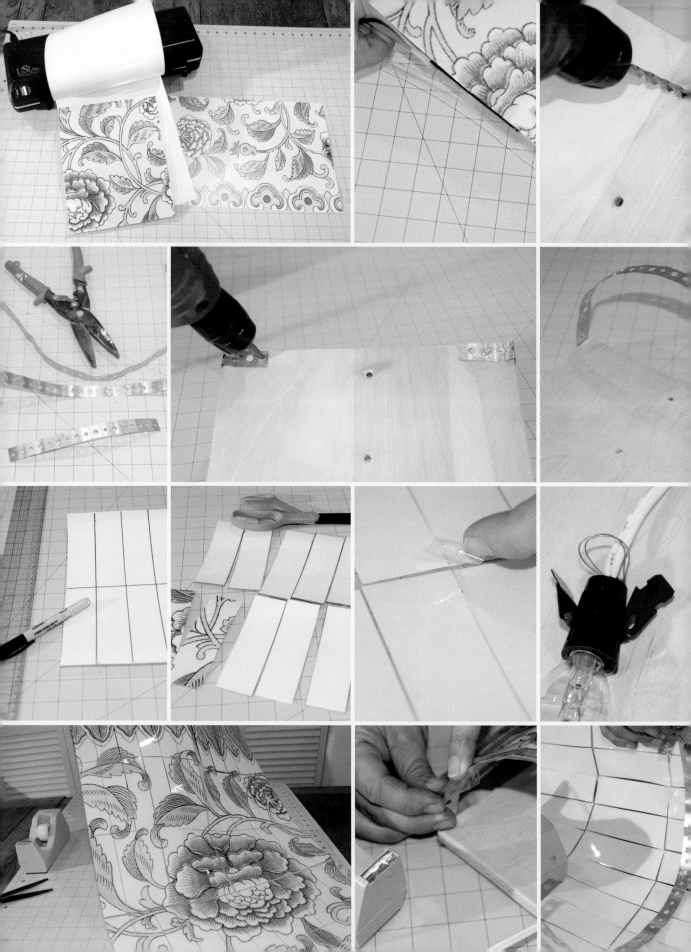

8. As you cut, tape the pieces together, leaving a tiny sliver of space between them. Tape at each intersection until you get all the way to the bottom. Once the entire image is back together, you'll see that it's very flexible.

9. Find a nail on the wall—or hammer one into the wall—and hang your wood piece so you can work easily.

10. Using a bread tie or small piece of wire, go through the hole in the back of the wood, wrap the wire around the socket-and-cord set, and secure in place.

11. Carefully attach the laminated image across the top piece of strapping using tape. Do the same with the bottom piece of strapping.

12. Add a bulb and plug in your fantastic creation. I know this one took a long time, but don't you love it?

CARDBOARD CHANDELIER

I don't care what anyone says about this cardboard chandelier. I love it! Using cardboard as a medium is fun and inexpensive—you can make as many mistakes as you want without feeling like you've wasted your money. On this project you're limited only by your imagination. Go wild and make something that will stop your friends in their tracks and make them compliment you on your genius.

YOU'LL NEED:

Three 10"-high plate stands

Amazing Goop Household glue

6' snap-in socket-and-cord set, with a switch on the cord and a candelabra base

Packing tape

Cardboard

Scissors

Hot glue gun and glue sticks

7' of rebar tie wire

Wire cutters

Newspaper

Krylon spray primer in white or gray

Krylon Fusion spray paint

Glitter glue (optional)

Toothpicks (optional)

15-watt chandelier bulb

HERE'S HOW:

1. Glue the three plate stands together (in their open position) with Goop and let them dry. This will be your chandelier base.

2. Add the socket-and-cord set by securing the socket in between the base of the plate stands and threading the cord up toward the top. Tape the cord in place in a crease between the plate stands.

3. Cut out lots of cardboard leaves and hot glue them up and down each side of the plate stands.

4. Cut out cardboard flowers as shown. I made about 16 of them for my chandelier.

5. Cut 5"-long pieces of rebar tie for the stems.

6. Hot glue the flowers to the ends of the rebar tie, and the other end of the wire to the chandelier.

7. Once you've glued all the leaves and flowers to the chandelier base and let them dry, put the whole thing on newspaper outdoors. Spray paint it with the primer, giving it a nice base for the color paint to stick to.

8. When the primer dries, spray paint the chandelier in the color you've chosen.

9. If you like, use toothpicks to add glitter glue to the flowers, just for fun. I mean, it's cardboard, so who cares?

10. Put in the bulb, plug it in, and you're done!

CALDER-ESQUE BUTTERFLY LAMP

Rebar wire is easy to bend and still keeps its shape, and it's really cheap. (You can find it at any hardware store.) It was perfect for this project! This lamp looks fantastic when all the other lights in the house are out because it throws amazing shadows. I hope you like it as much as I do and see the possibilities in it.

YOU'LL NEED:

1 roll of rebar tie wire

Yardstick

Wire cutters

Needle-nose pliers

6' snap-in socket-and-cord set, with a switch on the cord and a candelabra base

Empty 2-liter plastic bottle

Fine-point permanent marker

Scissors

Amazing Goop Household glue

Tape (optional)

Newspaper

Krylon Fusion spray paint in black

15-watt chandelier bulb

HERE'S HOW:

1. Cut a 24" piece of rebar tie and wrap it around the point of needle-nose pliers to make a spring.

2. With another piece of wire the same length, make squiggles.

3. Repeat the process until you have six or seven wire pieces to start putting together.

4. To connect them, clamp the end of a piece of bent wire around another one. Don't worry—there's no right or wrong way to make this lamp. It's all about what you like!

5. Wrap a 25" piece of wire around the cord of the socket set, starting about 3" above the socket and ending at the base of the socket.

6. Attach your springs and squiggles to the wire around the cord.

7. Create a cage of wires around the socket by clamping the ends of wires to other wires.

8. Next, wash out a 2-liter plastic bottle and cut it open. You'll be using the plastic for your butterfly shapes.

9. Draw butterflies on the plastic with a fine-point marker and cut them out with scissors. (If you're not sure how to draw a butterfly, just look for simple butterfly images on the Internet and copy them.)

10. Glue the butterflies to the wire cage. If you have to, tape them in place until they dry.

11. When everything looks the way you want it to, lay the lamp on newspaper outdoors. Spray paint the entire structure black.

12. Once it's dry, hang the lamp and put in the bulb. Switch it on, turn off all the other lights, and check out the shadows.

GEISHA FRINGE PENDANT LAMP

I am completely obsessed with anything Asian and anything with fringe. This hanging lamp marries the two perfectly. Also, I get tired of the same old hanging pendant lamp and this one actually dances when I turn on the AC. Movement, light, fringe, and Chinese red—I'm in heaven.

Thrift stores are the best places to get beat-up lampshades that you can strip the fabric from. I used a Victorian bell-shaped wire lampshade, but you could use any wire lampshade that is smaller at the top than it is at the bottom and has six to eight wires going all the way around. If you want a really great selection of wire lamp bases, check out lampshop.com. They have super-cool wire lamp bases and every component you need to make terrific lamps.

YOU'LL NEED:

Old lampshade frame (with at least 6 wires all the way around and tapered at the top)

Sandpaper

Rags

Newspaper

Krylon Fusion spray paint in red

1 yard of chain (or ribbon) to hang your lamp

Tin shears, wire cutters, or scissors

S-hook that fits through the link of the chain

Hot glue gun and glue sticks

Enough red fringe to cover all the wires on the lamp base plus 1 yard extra

Measuring tape

Elmer's Glue-All

6' snap-in socket-and-cord set, with a switch on the cord and a candelabra base

15-watt chandelier bulb

HERE'S HOW:

1. Clean the lampshade frame with sandpaper to create a good surface for the paint. Dust it off with a rag.

2. Set the frame on newspaper outdoors and spray paint it red.

3. Cut the chain (or ribbon) into three equal lengths.

4. Attach the chains equally spaced apart along the wide end of the base.

5. Connect the three chains at the top with the S-hook.

6. Put a dab of hot glue where the chain meets the wire base to keep it in place.

7. Hang the frame from an area in your home where you can work easily. I hooked mine on an open cabinet door handle.

8. Carefully hot glue the fringe (using very small dabs of hot glue!) on each wire all over the base.

9. With the extra yard of fringe, add one or two rings on the inside of the wire frame. Do this by stretching the fringe from wire to wire and dabbing Elmer's glue all around the fringe wherever it touches the frame. Don't worry—it will dry clear.

10. When the glue dries, hang the socket-and-cord set from the S-hook so the bulb sits nicely inside the lamp. Set the bulb in the socket and enjoy!

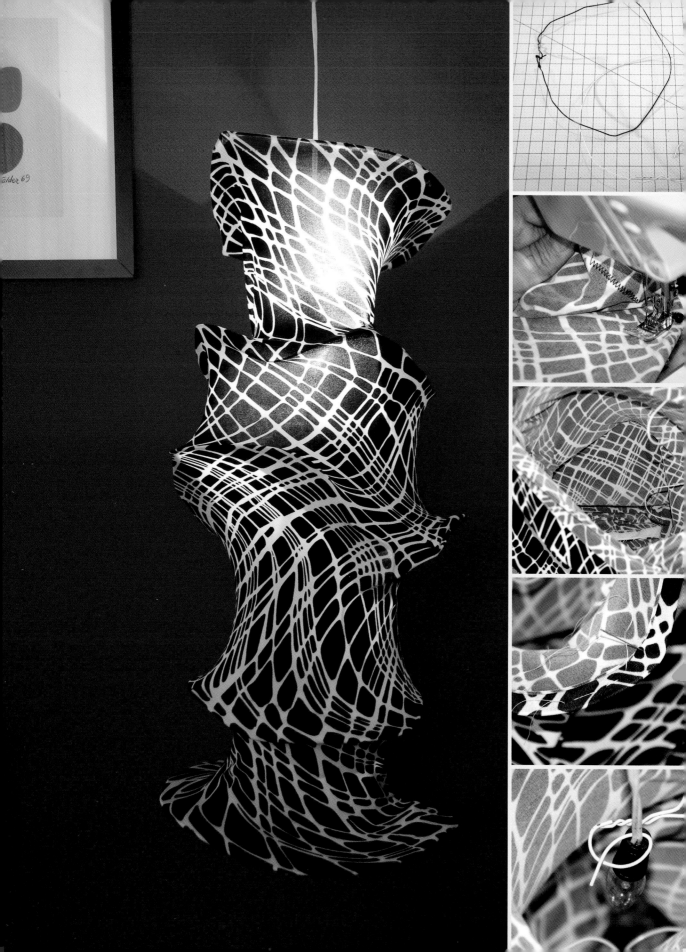

TWISTED LYCRA LAMP SCULPTURE

Since the dawn of time, wire hangers and stretchy fabric have gone together like Romeo and Juliet, like peanut butter and chocolate, like crayons and coloring books. I think this lamp looks like something Martha Graham would have had in her home. I love it with all its twists and turns. One word of caution, though: Your lamp will be totally different from mine, because there is no way two of these can be the same!

YOU'LL NEED:

3 wire hangers

Pliers

1 yard of super-stretchy Lycra or Spandex fabric

Scissors

Sewing machine and thread

Straight pins

Needle and thread

6' snap-in socket-and-cord set, with a switch on the cord and a candelabra base

15-watt chandelier bulb

HERE'S HOW:

1. Unwind and unbend the wire hangers so they're just long pieces of wire.

2. Cut the Lycra or Spandex to 20" x 36".

3. Fold it in half, long right sides together, and sew a 36"-long fabric tube.

4. Turn it right side out.

5. Bend each wire hanger into an 18"-diameter circle with the excess spiraling off.

6. Smoosh one wire circle and spiral inside the middle of the tube. Then put one wire circle at each end of the tube, with the circle parts toward the opening.

7. Position the end wires so that there is 1" of excess fabric on each end. This will be used to finish the edges later.

8. Use straight pins to keep all the wires in place.

9. With a needle and thread, stitch around the circle part of each wire to keep it in place so it doesn't move inside the tube.

10. Flip the 1" excess fabric inside each mouth of the lamp and tack it down with the needle and thread. This hides the wire and gives the sculpture a nice finished feel.

11. Bend one of the end spiraling wires toward the top of the lamp so it can wrap around the socket in the socket-and-cord set. Keep it in the center of the lamp—you don't want the lightbulb anywhere near the fabric!

12. Since this lamp is so light, it can easily hang from the socket-and-cord set. Just install a small hook and hang it. Put in the bulb, plug it in, and enjoy your glowing artwork!

GLASS CHIP PENDANT LAMP

I was in a restaurant once and saw beautiful lamps made of glass chips all over the ceiling. Although they were obviously made in Italy by a glassblower, I was totally inspired to make my own version with the supplies I have readily available in my craft room. These lamps can be made in different colors, with different shapes of glass chips—whatever you want. Just take your time, and when you're done, enjoy the beautiful light they give.

YOU'LL NEED:

Tough plastic container (not flexible)

Heavy-duty scissors (optional)

Drill with ¼" drill bit

Newspaper

Rags

Tons of glass chips in a color you like

Amazing Goop Household glue

Transparent tape

6' snap-in socket-and-cord set, with a switch on the cord and a candelabra base

15-watt chandelier bulb

HERE'S HOW:

1. If you need to, cut the rim off the plastic container so it has a nice clean edge.

2. Drill a hole in the center of the bottom so you have a place to wire the socket-and-cord set.

3. Lay down newspapers and pile up rags to keep the container from rolling around while you're gluing on the glass chips.

4. In groups of five or six, apply glue to the back of each glass chip and place it on the plastic.

5. To keep the chips in place until the glue sets, put tape over them for a few minutes.

6. Continue gluing on the glass chips until the entire container is covered. This may take a while since you'll have to wait until the glue sets each time you put on more chips.

7. Wire the socket set through the hole in the container, following the instructions that come with the set.

8. Screw in the bulb and hang from a hook.

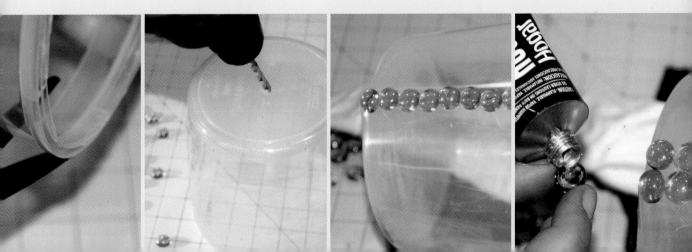

LUCITE PLATE-HOLDER CHANDELIER

I don't like to play favorites, but I have to say that this just may be my favorite project in the entire book. It's beautiful, simple, and easy to make. If I do say so myself, it was a stroke of crafty heaven when it finally came together.

YOU'LL NEED:

6 clear plastic plate stands (try the 99¢ store)

Newspaper

Pencil

Packing or masking tape

6' snap-in socket-and-cord set, with a switch on the cord and a candelabra base

Dremel tool with grinding attachment

Amazing Goop Household glue

15-watt chandelier bulb

HERE'S HOW:

1. Unfold three of the plate stands and arrange them, with legs touching, on a large piece of newspaper. Carefully mark on the newspaper where each of the legs touches—this is your guide.

2. Tape the three plate stands together. Take the socket set with the bulb screwed in and figure out how much space it will need on the inside of the chandelier (the bottom of the plate stands). Because the 6' socket set is so small, you probably won't need a lot of room.

3. With the Dremel tool, grind out enough space from all six legs so the bulb and socket will fit and you'll be able to wiggle out the bulb when it needs to be changed. I know this sounds difficult, but it's not. Just be patient and grind, baby, grind!

4. Using the guide you created on the newspaper, glue the first three plate stands together. The hinges are where mine fit together beautifully.

5. When the glue on the first three is dry, glue the other three together the same way.

6. When everything is dry, carefully slip in the socket with bulb and glue the two sets of plate stands together feet to feet.

7. With a dab of glue, attach the cord in a crease between two of the plate stands and hang the chandelier from a hook.

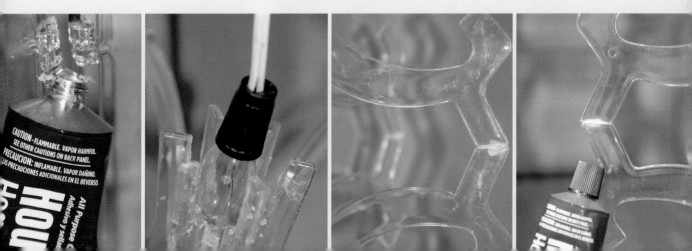

DECOUPAGE LAMP

Hey, we all have a lamp that needs some sprucing up. Though you've seen it again and again in different incarnations, this project is still a pretty cool way to make an old lamp look like a million bucks. The key to amazing decoupage is finding images that make your project sing. There are so many fantastic books out there with beautiful images, and many of them are inexpensive. I made this lamp in honor of my mother, who used to grow huge irises in the backyard, and the image came from a book on plants that I color copied at Staples. If you collect pictures that might look wonderful in a decoupage project, color copying is a great way to use them repeatedly.

YOU'LL NEED:

Color-copied images on 24 lb. paper (don't use lighter paper—it really won't work)

Scissors

Lamp with flat surfaces that are easy to adhere images to

Elmer's Glue-All

1"-wide paintbrush

Minwax Polycrylic Protective Finish (high gloss)

HERE'S HOW:

1. Copy enough images to cover the lamp base the way you want.

2. Carefully cut out the images. The more you pay attention to the details, the better it will look.

3. Position the images on your lamp base so you can visualize how they are going to look.

4. Water down Elmer's glue with a few drops of water so it can easily be brushed on with the paintbrush.

5. Brush the back of each image with the glue and apply it to the lamp. When you've attached all your images, let the glue dry.

6. Coat the entire lamp base with Polycrylic.

Suggestion: You can follow these instructions to decoupage anything from dressers to cabinet doors.

FABRIC GHOST LAMP

I'm naming this the Ghost Lamp because it's covered in white fabric. It reminds me of a kid who can't figure out what he wants to be for Halloween until the last minute, and then his mom has to get creative—and quick. I've got to say, though, that this is much cooler; in the right setting, it would look very modern and chic. Try this lamp with other fabrics like prints or stripes that match your room.

YOU'LL NEED:

Galvanized steel duct cap (any size will do; mine was 12" in diameter)

Tape measure

2 yards of lightweight fabric

Scissors

Sewing machine and thread

Two 1' lengths of ribbon (or shoe strings)

1 large safety pin

Drill with ¼" drill bit

6' snap-in socket-and-cord set, with a switch on the cord and a candelabra base

15-watt chandelier bulb

HERE'S HOW:

1. Measure the circumference of the duct cap and double it. (Mine was 27" around, so my measurement was 54".)

2. Decide how long you want your lamp to be (say, 5' long).

3. Cut out the fabric using the measurements in step 1 and step 2 (in this example, your piece will be 54" x 5').

4. With right sides together, sew along the length of the fabric using ½" seam allowance and make a very long tube. Flip the tube right side out.

5. Now you're going to create a channel for your ribbon. It gets a little tricky, but hold on—I'm right here with you! Fold in one end of the tube about 1½" and stitch 1¼" away from the fold, almost all the way around the circumference of the tube (leave a 1" opening).

6. Do the same on the other end of the tube. You've now created a drawstring tunnel at each end so you can smoosh the fabric together at the top and bottom.

7. Attach a safety pin to one piece of ribbon, thread it through the tunnel, and pull it to the other side. Repeat with the other ribbon in the second tunnel. Tie loose knots for now.

8. Drill a hole in the exact center of the duct cap so you can wire the socket-and-cord set. It's pretty easy—I use these sets all the time.

9. Once the socket-and-cord set is wired, slip one end of the fabric tube over the duct cap and pull the ribbon so the tube fits snuggly around the cord.

10. Put in the bulb.

11. Pull the ribbon at the bottom of the lamp, tie it, and tuck the ends inside the tube.

12. Hang the lamp from a hook and you're done! BOO!

BUTTERFLY CHANDELIER

Imagine your little girl looking up before she goes to sleep to see sparkling butterflies hovering above her head. This chandelier is perfect for any girl who loves sparkles, flowers, and butterflies—and don't they all? You don't even have to install a light in this chandelier if you don't want to; it's a beautiful piece all by itself.

YOU'LL NEED:

One 3- to 5-ring tomato cage from a garden store

Wire cutters

Sandpaper or sanding block

E-6000 glue

Hot glue gun and glue sticks

50' of cheap plastic pearls (try the 99¢ store)

Scissors

Ruler

Toothpicks

Newspaper

Krylon Crafter's Metallic spray paint in silver

12 feather butterflies

12 faux flowers

6' snap-in socket-and-cord set, with a switch on the cord and a candelabra base (optional)

15-watt chandelier bulb (optional)

Hint: When working with small objects like pearls or glass chips, use toothpicks to dab on glue instead of squeezing it from the tube. It's a lot neater that way.

HERE'S HOW:

1. Clip the larger rings off the tomato cage with your wire cutters, leaving two rings connected by extended wires.

2. Sand the wires to remove any dirt, rust, or oil.

3. Bend the wires extending from the small ring of the cage into curlicues, facing out, as you see in the photo.

4. Bend the wires extending from the large ring toward the center so they meet. Glue these wires together where they meet with a big glob of E-6000 glue.

5. Hot glue strings of pearls along each wire of the now-bent cage. (Hot glue and metal don't work well together, so you're just using this to hold the pearls in place for the next step.)

6. Once the strands are in place, carefully dab E-6000 glue all along the pearls so they're permanently attached.

7. Cut six strands of pearls 12" long. Hot glue both ends of each strand to the top ring so you have two drapes between each wire. Don't worry—this is the fun part. Just start draping any way you want to and you'll see how beautiful it can be.

8. After you've attached the six strands, dab on more E-6000 with a toothpick, being very neat but making sure to attach the end pearls to the wire with the glue.

9. Once the pearls are in place, put the chandelier on newspaper outdoors and spray paint it.

10. When it's dry, attach butterflies and flowers evenly all the way around, first with hot glue and then with E-6000. I used 12 butterflies and 12 flowers, but go crazy if you want to.

11. *Optional:* Wrap the socket-and-cord set around the top where the wires meet and hang it from a hook in your ceiling. Sweet dreams!

HOBO CHIC LAMP BASE AND SHADE

If you're anything like me, you can't seem to toss out even the smallest scrap of fabric or the shortest piece of ribbon. I have bags of them waiting to be used for something. I call this lamp Hobo Chic because it almost didn't matter what scraps I used, as long as the colors and patterns worked well together. You might even try squares or triangles to make the lamp look like a quilt. Just keep saving those scraps and, like me, you'll eventually find a great use for them.

YOU'LL NEED:

Scraps of fabric, enough to cover the lamp base and shade

Pinking shears

Newspaper

Lamp and lampshade in serious need of an overhaul

Minwax Polycrylic Protective Finish

1"-wide paintbrush

Pencil

Scissors

HERE'S HOW:

To make the lamp base:

1. Decide what fabric shapes you're going to use for your lamp. This is important, because once you start applying the fabric, your fingers will be sticky and it will be hard to cut more shapes without making a huge mess. I chose fabric strips, but you could use squares or triangles.

2. Cut the fabric into your desired shapes with pinking shears (the shears give more texture and interest than scissors do). Make sure you've cut all the pieces you'll need to use before you start applying them to the base.

3. Place the lamp on newspaper on top of your workspace.

4. Using the paintbrush, coat the back of the scraps with the Polycrylic and apply them to the lamp.

5. Add more Polycrylic to the fabric once it's adhered to the base.

6. Repeat steps 4 and 5 until the entire lamp is covered.

7. For interest, add some strips of fabric around the base of the lamp and around the neck.

To make the lampshade:

1. Place the lampshade on its seam at the edge of a clean sheet of newspaper.

2. Roll the shade along and trace the top and bottom edge of the shade to make a lampshade pattern.

3. Cut out the pattern.

Instructions continue on next two pages.

4. Divide the lampshade pattern into 8 equal sections by folding it in half, then half again, then half again. If you unfold the pattern, you'll see that it's creased into 8 equal parts. To make things easier, though, just use the folded paper as your pattern.

5. Cut 8 pieces of fabric following your paper pattern.

6. Starting at the seam, apply the fabric pieces by painting the fabric back with Polycrylic and then adhering it to the shade. Add another coat of the Polycrylic to the outside of the fabric. Apply the fabric pieces all the way around the shade.

7. Cut small strips (about ⅜" wide) of fabric to create a ribbon effect between the different fabric panels, and apply them with the Polycrylic.

8. To finish the top and bottom of the shade, cut a ½"-wide strip of fabric on the bias. If you need to use more than one strip for each rim, don't worry—it will only increase the patchwork quality of the project. Attach the strips with the Polycrylic all the way around and let dry.

Hint: In case you don't know what bias is, pretend you have a perfect square of fabric. If you fold it in half to create a triangle, the length of the fold is the bias. When you cut fabric on the bias, it has stretch. Pretty cool, right?

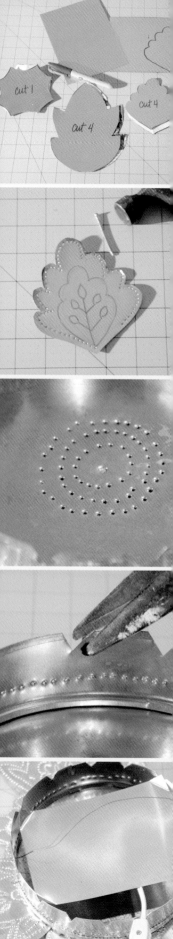

TAPPED-ALUMINUM WALL SCONCE

Aluminum roof flashing is amazing, and I often find ways to use it in my craft projects. It's durable and beautiful, and you can paint and tap it like crazy. This project is pure hardware store, but it looks like a million bucks.

YOU'LL NEED:

Templates on page 260

Paper

Pencil

Scissors

9 pieces of 7" x 5" aluminum roof flashing or about 2' of 12"-wide aluminum flashing on a roll

Heavy-duty scissors or tin shears

Scrap wood

2 large nails for tapping

Small hammer

8" galvanized steel duct cap

Transparent tape

Amazing Goop Household glue

Small pieces of cardboard

3' of small-gauge wire

6' snap-in socket-and-cord set, with a switch on the cord and a candelabra base

15-watt chandelier bulb

HERE'S HOW:

1. With a pencil, draw the template patterns onto the flashing: Draw four of the large leaf, four of the medium leaf, two of the small leaf, and one of the center piece. Cut out all the pieces with heavy-duty scissors.

2. Set the cut pieces of flashing on the piece of scrap wood and tap your designs with a large nail and small hammer.

3. When you're done tapping your designs on the flashing, place the duct cap on the scrap wood. Tap out holes all the way around the circumference and top of the duct cap; this will allow light to come through.

4. Cut out small triangles from around the rim of the duct cap to let even more light shine through.

5. Once you've completed all the tapping and cutting, tape the large leaf designs onto the top of the duct cap at the positions of 12, 3, 6, and 9 on a clock face. When the leaves are where you want them, glue them on with the Goop glue.

6. Build up a few small pieces of cardboard into a stack. Glue the pieces onto the center of the duct cap, then glue the center piece on top, so it hovers above the large leaves.

7. Glue the four medium leaves between the large leaves.

8. Tuck the two small leaves at the top and bottom of the center piece and glue in place.

9. When the glue is dry, cut an 8" piece of small-gauge wire and string it through two of the holes you've tapped in the duct cap to make a hanging wire.

10. String another 8" piece of wire through the sides of the duct cap and use it to hang the small light socket.

11. Cut one more piece of aluminum flashing so it fits on the back of the sconce and tape it into place with clear tape. This will keep the bulb from touching the wall.

12. Screw in the bulb and hang up the sconce.

H. P. LOVECRAFT CHANDELIER

I have five fantastic brothers who are all super talented and very supportive of my life. My brother Phil is always thinking of me when he hits junk sales and thrift stores. For my birthday last year he sent me an old chandelier to use as a project in this book. I have to say, when I opened the box I wasn't inspired. But I still made sure to tell him how much I appreciated what he had done. I left the chandelier on my kitchen table for a month and then it finally hit me . . . *octopus!* I found tiny glass chips at Michaels and went to town. When in doubt, folks, get out the glue! H. P. Lovecraft is a science fiction writer and I'm almost sure he had a chandelier like this in his house.

YOU'LL NEED:

Chandelier

Old towels

Small glass chips to cover the chandelier (about 8 bags)

E-6000 glue

Tape

Toothpicks

Krylon Fusion spray paint (optional)

HERE'S HOW:

1. Clean your chandelier thoroughly to get all the dirt off. Remove the faux candles, bulbs, and any little pieces of wire that may have been left behind from its former life.

2. Pile the towels on your workspace in a clump and set the chandelier on top to keep it stable while you glue.

3. Working along one side, glue on a line of glass chips in a row, keeping them in place with tape if you have to. It will take about 10 minutes for the glue to set before you can work on the next row, so be patient. Use toothpicks to get small amounts of glue on the chips; it's easier than squeezing large amounts from the end of the tube.

4. In order for the chandelier to look terrific, glue on the chips the same way on each arm. This means you'll copy that first line of glass chips on each arm of the chandelier as you glue. You'll get the hang of it.

5. *Optional:* If you've chosen colored glass chips, spray paint the faux candles in a color that matches. I chose a dark hot pink since my chips were reddish pink. Take a step back and make sure you didn't miss any spots.

6. Either make this a plug-in chandelier that you can hang from a hook, or have an electrician come in and wire it up for you.

Hint: When working with small objects like pearls or glass chips, use toothpicks to dab on glue instead of squeezing it from the tube. It's a lot neater that way.

TAPPED-TIN WATER-HEATER PAN SCONCE

While walking through The Home Depot one day, I was literally overcome by the need to have this water-heater pan. I have no idea why—it just screamed out, "TAKE ME HOME!" So I did. This is what happened. Don't you think this light is amazing?

YOU'LL NEED:

Water-heater pan

Paper

Scissors

Permanent marker

Hammer

Large nails

Flat piece of scrap wood

4' of small-gauge wire or picture-hanging wire

6' snap-in socket-and-cord set, with a switch on the cord and a candelabra base

25-watt lightbulb

HERE'S HOW:

1. Cut out a piece of paper the size of your water-heater pan.

2. Fold it in half and then half again.

3. Cut out a crazy design on it and unfold it. It's kind of like cutting out a snowflake but not as complicated.

4. Place the cutout on the inside of the pan with one of the folds directly above the hole in the pan.

5. Trace around the cutout with a permanent marker.

6. Refold the same cutout and cut a new design, removing about 1 ½" of the original edge.

7. Place the new cutout on the inside of the pan and trace around it with the marker.

8. Repeat steps 6 and 7 to make an even smaller cutout that will fit inside the first two.

9. Place the water-heater pan on the scrap wood and follow your tracings with a hammer and nail, making small holes a little less than ¼" apart. Continue until you've tapped all 3 of the designs onto the pan.

10. Tap two holes on opposite sides of the pan (leaving the pre-existing hole at the bottom).

11. Thread the small-gauge wire through the holes on the sides so you have something to hang your sconce.

12. Thread the plug through the hole at the bottom of the sconce.

13. Screw in the lightbulb and hang on the wall.

BLACK RIBBON LAMPSHADE

I really dig this translucent lampshade—it has a very Addams Family look. When I was working on the plaster-dipped flower lamp base (see page 96), I knew I would need a good shade for it, but I couldn't find one to save my soul. So, like any crafter worth his glue gun, I took matters into my own hands and this is what happened. Try this lampshade using strips of really cool fabric cut with pinking shears. Or experiment with this technique using different colors of ribbon, Mardi Gras beads, even yarn or twine. It's easy and addicting—and will always yield terrific results.

YOU'LL NEED:

Hot glue gun and glue sticks

14 yards of 1½"- to 2"-wide ribbon

Wire lampshade frame

Scissors

14 yards of ¾"-wide ribbon

3 yards of black bias tape

HERE'S HOW:

1. With your lampshade in place on top of the base, carefully hot glue lengths of the 1½" ribbon from the top wire of the shade to the bottom wire. Pull the ribbon tight and hold it in place until the glue sets, then trim the excess.

2. Apply the second piece of ribbon next to the first. Since most shades are tapered, you'll have to overlap the ribbon pieces a bit more at the top than at the bottom. Square shades are easy; you just start at the center of the shade and work your way out. With curved shades you have to make sure that each of the ribbon pieces is going straight up and down, and they will naturally overlap more at the top.

3. When you've finished gluing the ribbon around the entire lamp, glue on pieces of the ¾"-wide ribbon between the 1½"-wide pieces. This gives a great effect.

4. After you've glued on the two types of ribbon, cover the top and bottom edges of the shade by hot gluing the black bias tape all the way around.

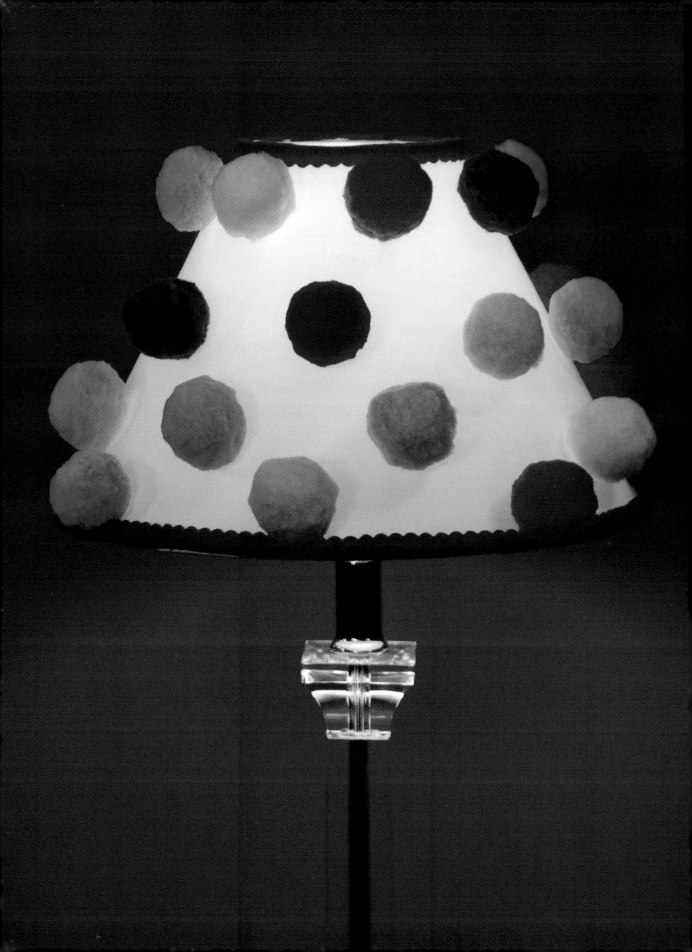

KIDS' PUFFBALL LAMPSHADE

I'm a big kid. Kids' crafts are the most fun to make because they're colorful and zany—which is just how my mother describes me! (Well, she uses a few other words, too, but those are not appropriate for a craft book.) Puffballs are amazing; at age 10 I would have much preferred a treasure trunk filled with these bundles of joy rather than jewels. Stick them on anything from pillows to curtain edges and watch your inner child emerge.

YOU'LL NEED:

Bright-colored felt that matches one of the puffballs

Pinking shears

Hot glue gun and glue sticks

Lampshade in white fabric (or bright yellow or green!)

30 puffballs in different colors

HERE'S HOW:

1. Cut ½"-wide strips of felt with your pinking shears to create your own edging for the lampshade.

2. Hot glue the felt around the top and bottom rims of the shade.

3. Decide where to place the puffballs before you begin gluing. Then glue them on carefully one by one until you've covered the entire shade. Now that was easy, wasn't it?

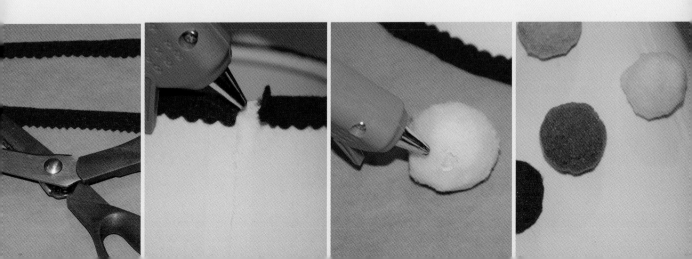

SCRAP-RIBBON LAMPSHADE

I didn't really plan on making this lampshade, but the scrap ribbon bin in my craft room was starting to overflow. I save every little scrap, button, or swatch I can get my hands on. It's a habit I've never been able to break! In the case of this project, it worked out well for me. Because of its many colors, this lampshade will look good in any room. Lets face it: If I had a kitchen sink to glue on it, I probably would have.

I like using braided or flexible trim for the top and bottom edge of a lampshade because it conforms to the shape more easily than other trims. And using ribbon can get very tricky. Honestly, I'm just not that good at it . . . yet.

YOU'LL NEED:

Lampshade in need of some crafty lovin'

Hot glue gun and glue sticks

Scraps of ribbon at least the length of the shade

Braided trim for the top and bottom of the shade

HERE'S HOW:

1. Start at the top of your lampshade and, using a very thin line of hot glue across the rim, attach one end of ribbon.

2. Stretch the ribbon down and glue the other end to the bottom rim. You don't have to glue on the rest of the ribbon—just the top and bottom edges. It works better this way.

3. Starting at the top of the shade again, overlap the next ribbon a bit. Glue it in place at the top rim, take it straight down to the bottom of the shade, and glue it to the bottom rim. You're getting the hang of it now! Continue until you've got ribbon all the way around the shade.

4. When all the ribbons are glued on, hot glue the braided trim around the top and bottom rims of the shade to cover all the raw edges.

5. Put this shade in any room of your home. Trust me: It will find a way to match.

DYED TWINE LAMPSHADE

OK, I know you're saying you've seen this before . . . and you have. But I've added a twist to it! Did you know you can *dye* twine? It takes color quite beautifully. So next time you see a big fat roll of twine in the 99¢ store (where I got mine), you'll know it doesn't have to remain that beige color. You can dye it whatever color you want and it will look amazing. I chose Ranger Color Wash in a color called Lettuce for this lampshade. You need to check out their products—they're really cool!

YOU'LL NEED:

Old lampshade with all the paper and cloth removed

Large roll of twine

Hot glue gun and glue sticks

Newspaper

1 bottle Ranger Color Wash spray

HERE'S HOW:

1. Wrap the top and bottom wires of your lampshade with twine, dabbing little bits of hot glue along the wire to keep it in place.

2. Circle the entire shade with twine, starting at the bottom or top and working your way up or down. Use hot glue to attach the twine where it meets the wires, and dab a bit here and there to glue one row of twine to another as you go along.

3. When you're finished with the wrapping, place your shade on newspaper outdoors and spray inside and out with Color Wash.

4. Allow the shade to dry and then pop it on a lamp!

CHAPTER 9

BRILLIANT BEDROOMS

This may be a tiny chapter, but who cares? The fact is that the three projects in this chapter can be made in a thousand different ways. It's up to you to figure out how to make them work with your décor. What I want you to do is to **blast bedroom boredom,** but I don't mean what you may think I mean. I want you to take these bed projects and a few of the other projects in this book and **spruce up that room** where you spend nearly a third of your life. Make it beautiful so at the end of the day **you have a terrific place to sleep.** Make your bed **comfortable** and **inviting** and—who knows?—you may end up blasting your bedroom boredom **with someone** as terrific as you!

PADDED FRAME HEADBOARD

This is a quick way to make an elegant headboard if you don't have one. What's more, it's easy to change out when you get tired of it—one of the main reasons I love making these headboards for friends on a budget.

YOU'LL NEED:

3 large picture frames that together total the width of your bed

2 yards of fabric

Scissors

2 yards of batting (flat stuffing used for quilting)

Heavy-duty packing tape

Hammer and nails

HERE'S HOW:

1. Remove the glass and paper from your frames—you won't need them. You will need the hard piece of board that fits on the back of the frame though, so don't toss that! Let's call that the frame back.

2. Lay one of the frame backs on the fabric, add 3 inches to each side all the way around, and cut the fabric.

3. Cut two more pieces of fabric the same size.

4. Lay the first frame back on the batting and cut around it exactly. Cut two more the same way.

5. Place a piece of batting on the frame back and lay the fabric over it evenly.

6. Wrap the edge of the fabric around the frame back and use the heavy-duty packing tape to attach it firmly.

7. Put this piece into the frame and secure it in place with the metal stays that originally secured the frame back to the frame.

8. Repeat this process with the other frames.

9. Figure out where on the wall you want to position the frames, then attach with hammer and nails. I would suggest that you actually nail the frames to the wall rather than hang them on the wall. This will really keep them in place.

10. Change the fabric when you redecorate your room.

BLOCK-PRINTED SUZANI BLANKET

Suzani tapestries originated in Uzbekistan, and no one knows how long ago this tradition of embroidery began. (Suzani means "needle" in the Persian language.) I've always loved these embroidered tapestries, but they're quite expensive. So I decided to make my own version with cork stamps and paint colors that match my bedroom. Just look up Suzani on the Internet, and you'll be as inspired as I was.

There's no need for perfection here! I mean it. I splattered, overlapped, smudged, you name it . . . and I love the way it looks. I used acrylic latex paint in red, black, and rust, which you can find in any craft store. You can also use paint left over from painting your room, as long as it's water-based (latex)—don't use oil-based paint.

YOU'LL NEED:

Cork stamps (see page 90) using Suzani templates on page 261

1 beige flat sheet in your bed size

Iron and ironing board

Newspaper

Ruler

String

Pencil

Water-based paint (I used black, red, and rust)

¾"-wide paintbrush

Black ribbon and sewing machine (optional)

HERE'S HOW:

1. Create your Suzani cork stamps following the instructions on page 90 and using the templates provided. Feel free to change the shapes up a bit to make them your very own.

2. Divide the flat sheet into nine equal squares by folding it in thirds lengthwise and then in thirds widthwise.

3. Iron on the folds of the sheet so you can see the nine squares when you unfold it.

4. Open the sheet on a large flat workspace covered with newspaper. To make a nice circle, tie a string around a pencil and cut the string to 10 inches. Anchor the end of the string with your finger in the center square in the middle of the sheet. Stretch the pencil to the end of the string and draw a 20"-diameter circle all the way around. (Or you can just trace around a 20" round object instead.)

5. Paint cork stamp A with black paint using a ¾" brush and stamp your first circle of patterns onto the sheet.

6. Paint stamp B with red paint and stamp the red center.

7. Paint stamp C with black paint and stamp a circle 3" out from the first large circle, making sure to leave room for the flowers in between.

8. Paint stamp D with rust paint and stamp the flowers between the designs you made with stamp C.

Instructions continue on next two pages.

9. Paint stamp B with red paint and stamp a larger circle around the flower circle.

10. Paint stamp E with black paint and stamp all the way around the edges of the folded square.

11. Paint stamp F with black paint and stamp in each corner.

12. Let dry for a few minutes and start on your next square.

13. Just for fun and texture, I sewed black ribbon between the squares, but you don't have to.

14. When the entire sheet is dry, lightly press it with a dry iron to set the paint. Wait about 1 week before you wash your beautiful new Suzani.

FAUX INTARSIA HEADBOARD

I love the Internet because it offers so much you can use for reference. When I wanted to make a heraldic lion image on my headboard, I went to Google, typed in "images" and "heraldic lion," and voila—at least 50 to choose from. I also wanted to add my initial, so I looked up the letter M and found one that I like very much.

For this project I also used something even my mother knows about, a machine for scrapbookers called the Cricut Expression (check it out at www.provocraft.com). You can load it with various cartridges for fonts and shapes, which it then prints and cuts out perfectly. I started playing with it and now I'm totally hooked. I've found tons of different ways to use it for everything from stencils to this headboard. I'm in love!

YOU'LL NEED:

Images

2' of wood-grain contact paper (most hardware chains have it in shades from light to dark)

Light box or window

Fine-point permanent marker

Cutting mat or cardboard

Craft knife

Flat headboard

Yardstick

Pencil

Cricut Expression (optional; for the more intricate headboard)

HERE'S HOW:

1. Find a heraldic lion and your initial on the Internet and print them out as large as you can. I was able to print my lion to fill an entire 8 ½" x 11" sheet of paper.

2. Place the lion under the contact paper (with the backing still in place) on a light box or sunny window and trace the design using a fine-point marker. Do the same with your initial.

3. Carefully cut out the designs with a craft knife on a cutting mat or cardboard so you don't damage your tabletop.

4. Find the exact center of the headboard and the exact center of the initial, peel off the contact paper backing, and stick the letter to the headboard.

5. With the backing still on the lion, move it around the headboard to see where you want to place it. Mark the position lightly with a pencil.

6. Peel and stick the lion to the headboard.

To make the more intricate headboard:

You'll need the Cricut Expression and the font cartridge called Blackletter, which has Old English letters and some terrific shapes from which to choose.

1. Place the contact paper on the cutting mat and load the Cricut Expression following the instructions.

2. Cut the shapes you like to about 2 ½" according to the Cricut.

3. Follow steps 2, 3, 5, and 6 above, sticking the shapes wherever you want to add more pizzazz to your headboard.

CHAPTER 10

MARVELOUS MIRRORS

People may think I'm vain because **I have a lot of mirrors** in my home. Well, I'm not! I have so many of them because I live in a 500-square-foot apartment in New York City, where **the illusion of space is just as important as actually having it.** Mirrors make all the difference in **making a room seem larger** or **reflecting light** into an area of your home that's dark and gloomy. A mirror can **pretend to be a window** when it's placed across from an actual window on an otherwise boring wall. **The reflection will fool you every time.** I'm not sure how I feel about feng shui, because no matter how much I've been warned against placing something in a certain spot, chances are it's going to stay there if I like it. Fact is, there is **nothing lovelier** than beautiful mirrors dotted around a home, even if your friends do think you're **conceited.** Truth be told, I am a little vain, but that's only because **my mom always told me I was the most handsome boy in the world.** Naturally, I believe every word she says.

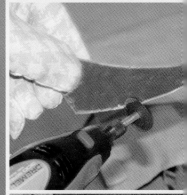

VENETIAN GLASS MIRROR

I've tried this style of mirror over and over again, and I think I've finally got it down. This technique is much easier than mosaic, which is what I first attempted (see page 188). Now, you might think that broken glass is hard to work with, but it's not. Just wear gloves and eye goggles. We are not taking risks here! So you must use goggles, not safety glasses—I mean it! Also, I'm letting you know now that your mirror will end up looking different from mine. It's an organic project, and that's what makes it wonderful.

YOU'LL NEED:

2 small screws and picture-hanging wire

12" x 24" piece of ½" plywood

Six 12"-square mirror tiles
(2 for mirrors and 4 to break)

E-6000 glue

Eye goggles

Gloves

Paper grocery bag

Hammer

Dremel tool with grinding attachment

1 bag of clear glass chips
(if you want a color, go for it!)

Safety Note: Always wear goggles that cover the entire eye area (not safety glasses) when you're working with glass or mirror pieces.

HERE'S HOW:

1. Before you start making this project, put two screws on the back of the plywood and wrap picture-hanging wire between them so you can hang the mirror when you're done.

2. Glue two mirror tiles to the plywood using E-6000 glue. This is the base of the mirror. Yes, there's a seam in the middle, but who cares? This is a craft project!

3. Put on your goggles and gloves. Place one mirror tile at a time in a paper bag and smash it with a hammer. Don't smash it too much because you do want some large pieces. If you hit it right in the middle, you'll get some wonderfully shaped shards.

4. Pour out the pieces and start to grind their edges with the Dremel tool. This is going to take a little while, but I assure you it takes much less time than mosaic—and the results make it all worthwhile.

5. Start gluing pieces all the way around the frame in a decorative manner. You can decide the design as you go; try different things. *Hint:* Save the smaller pieces for covering up the mirror frame and the longer shards for decorating the top center and sides to create a crown effect.

6. Once you've glued pieces all the way around the edge of the mirror, add the longer shards and smaller pieces. While gluing, remember to completely cover the edges of the mirror so it will truly have the effect of a Venetian mirror, which is all glass.

7. To give your mirror more shape, use the larger pieces to extend your design at the top and bottom.

8. It's time to glue on the glass chips—go crazy! Keep going until you've achieved your look.

9. Let the mirror dry and hang it with pride.

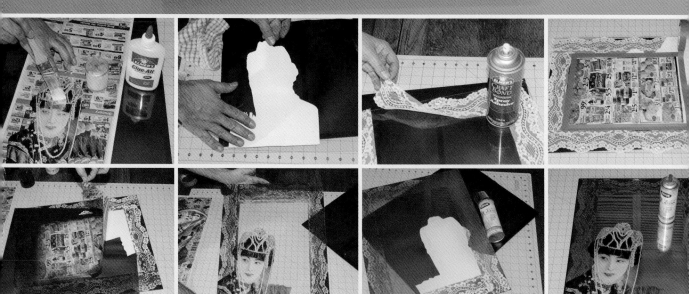

DECOUPAGE MIRROR

I've always been a huge fan of antique Chinese mirrors. You know—the ones with the beautiful paintings on the reverse. I finally figured out how to make my own version, and now I'm making them with every image I can get my hands on. Staples is the only place I've found that can make high-quality copies in the size you'll need. (Ask for 24 lb. paper.) The other thing that makes this mirror possible is Krylon's amazing Looking Glass paint, which will turn any clear glass surface into a mirror. Once I found out about it, my whole crafty world turned upside down. You're going to flip for this project too.

YOU'LL NEED:

For the mirror with lace:

Frame with glass the size you want your mirror

Elmer's Glue-All

1"-wide paintbrush

Color-copied image on 24 lb. paper that fits inside the frame

Scissors

2 yards of 3"-wide polyester lace trim

Elmer's Craft Bond Spray Adhesive

Newspaper

Masking tape

Krylon Fusion spray paint in red

Krylon Looking Glass spray paint

To make a mirror without lace, skip steps 5 to 9. You won't need the lace, spray adhesive, masking tape, or red paint.

HERE'S HOW:

1. Take the frame apart, remove the glass, and save the cardboard and the backing.

2. Water down Elmer's glue a little so it spreads easily with the paintbrush.

3. Cut out your color-copied image.

4. Paint glue on the face of the image and stick it to the glass.

5. Cut the lace into pieces so it can be placed around the edge of the frame as you see in the photo.

6. Coat the lace with spray adhesive and adhere it to the glass.

7. Set the glass on newspaper outdoors. Using clean newspaper and masking tape, cover the center of the mirror and just the inner edge of the lace.

8. Spray the lace with the red spray paint.

9. When it dries, remove the paper and the lace.

10. Spray a light coat of the Looking Glass paint on the glass and let it dry. Apply several more coats, waiting 4 minutes or so between coats.

11. Turn the glass over to see if you've applied enough paint to make it reflective.

12. Once you've achieved the amount of reflection you want, put the glass in the frame and cover the back with the protective piece of cardboard.

13. Place the backing on the frame and hang.

TONY DUQUETTE—INSPIRED MIRROR

Tony Duquette is one of my all-time favorite interior artists. He's been an inspiration to me for years. Look him up when you have a chance and you'll see why. He was a master of arts and crafts; the man knew how to have a good time with plaster of Paris. He was also known to spend thousands of dollars at 99¢ stores for his projects—something we have in common. This mirror is an homage to him.

     I painted the mirror about four times before I got it to where I wanted it. I love the turquoise and gold together, but I'm going to try a few other colors with the gold as well. If the list of items seems weird to you, feel free to change it up and make it your own. Don't worry if you don't have pearls or even fringe. You'll make it happen. The important thing to remember when making this mirror is that nothing is set in stone. It's all about the process, and the final product will look great no matter what.

YOU'LL NEED:

Template on page 261

12"-square piece of ¼" plywood

Fine-point permanent marker

Jigsaw

1 yard of cotton fabric

Scissors

12" of 10"-wide aluminum flashing to make feathers (or use real feathers!)

Tin shears

Mirror you want to decorate

Two ½" wood screws

Drill or screwdriver

Masking tape

Newspaper

Hot glue gun and glue sticks

2 ceramic birds (try the 99¢ store)

Plaster of Paris

Large mixing bowl

Rubber gloves (optional)

3 yards of fake plastic pearls

Amazing Goop Household glue

Elmer's Wood Glue

100 small buttons (or glass chips or beads)

3 small pinecones or faux flowers

1 yard of heavy fringe

Krylon Crafter's Metallic spray paint in gold

Benjamin Moore flat paint in turquoise (or any other color)

2"-wide paintbrush

1"-wide paintbrush

HERE'S HOW:

1. Trace the fleur-de-lis template onto the plywood, and cut out the shape with a jigsaw.

2. Cut the fabric into 12"-wide strips.

3. Draw four or five 10"-high feather shapes onto the flashing and cut them out using tin shears.

Instructions continue on next two pages.

cut !
in plywood

Plaster
of Paris
Yeso de Paris

4. Carefully screw the fleur-de-lis piece to the back top of the mirror frame so it extends about 9" above the mirror.

5. Lean the mirror up against a wall and tape newspaper over the front so you don't get plaster and paint on it while you work.

6. Hot glue the birds to the top of the mirror frame. Be generous with the glue.

7. Prepare the plaster of Paris in the large mixing bowl using very cold water. (Wear rubber gloves if you like.) You have to work fast here!

8. Dip the fabric strips in the plaster. Drape two strips over the top of the mirror—making two swags—and wrap them around the sides. Experiment with the wrapping until you get it the way you want it.

9. Drape the third strip of fabric around the neck of the fleur-de-lis and tuck it into the first drape.

10. Once the plaster is dry, drape and glue on the plastic pearls using the hot glue gun.

11. Using the Goop glue, attach the feathers to the top back of the fleur-de-lis and, if it works with the birds you bought, onto their tails.

12. With the Elmer's glue, attach the buttons around the fleur-de-lis. If you don't have buttons, use beads, pinecones, faux flowers, glass chips, or fringe—whatever you'd like.

13. Once everything is dry, set the mirror outdoors on newspaper and spray paint it with the metallic gold paint. When you do this, you'll see how great it's going to look.

14. With the 2" brush, spread flat paint on everything except the birds and the pearls, and leave some gold peeking through.

15. If you need more gold, spray some on an old paintbrush and brush it where it's needed.

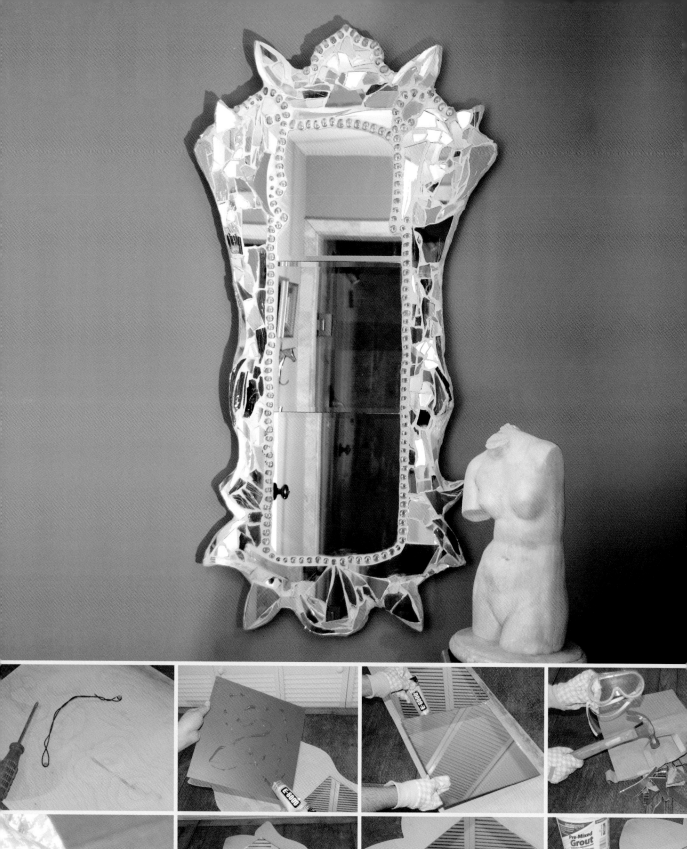

MOSAIC MIRROR

If you've ever seen a mosaic mirror, you know how beautiful—and expensive—they can be. As much as I love them, I thought it would be more fun just to make one that echoed the style. I was fortunate enough to find a discarded wardrobe mirror on my street. Despite the fact that it was a broken mirror, I think I was pretty lucky with the results.

YOU'LL NEED:

Three 12"-square mirror tiles

2' x 4' sheet of ½"-thick plywood

Fine-point permanent marker

Jigsaw

Two ½" screws

Picture-hanging wire

E-6000 glue

Gloves

Eye goggles

Broken mirror pieces or 4 broken mirror tiles

Paper grocery bag

Hammer

Dremel tool with grinding attachment

Glass chips to line the inside of the mirror and perhaps make a design

Bathroom tile grout

Sponge

Large bowl of cold water

HERE'S HOW:

1. Lay out the three mirror tiles in the center of the plywood.

2. Draw a design of your choice around the mirror tiles.

3. Remove the mirror tiles from the wood and cut out your design with a jigsaw.

4. Put the 2 screws in the back of the wood and wrap the wire between them so you can hang the mirror when it's finished. (Because of all the glass, this mirror can be heavy.)

5. Glue down the three mirror tiles with the E-6000.

6. Put the extra or broken mirror tiles in a paper bag, put on your goggles and gloves, and smash them to create small pieces.

7. With your Dremel and grinding attachment, go over the edges of the broken glass pieces so they can't cut you. This is quick and easy once you get the hang of it.

8. Start gluing the mirror pieces on the raw wood around the mirror tiles with E-6000. (If you need smaller pieces, put the large pieces in a paper bag and tap with a hammer.)

9. Once you've glued all the broken pieces around the 3 mirror tiles, glue glass chips along the edges of the tiles.

10. When all the pieces are in place and the glue has dried, fill in the spaces with grout. Squeeze a generous amount of grout between all the glass pieces. When you have a 5"-square area covered, wipe the excess grout off with a damp sponge. Don't worry if you have grout residue on the mirror; you can wipe it off after it dries.

Safety Note: Always wear goggles that cover the entire eye area (not safety glasses) when you're working with glass or mirror pieces.

RED-AND-GOLD LACE MIRROR

This lace and spray paint technique works on almost anything. I needed a mirror with some punch and was tired of the same old wood-framed ones. This mirror had a terrific raised dot detail and some wonderful crevices that were perfect for running my gold paint pen along. The only thing that might make this project even more fabulous is some black-and-white zebra ribbon around the edge!

YOU'LL NEED:

Blue painter's tape

Newspaper

Large mirror with at least a 3"-wide frame

Krylon Crafter's Metallic spray paint in gold

Scissors

1 yard of lace

Elmer's Craft Bond Spray Adhesive

Krylon Fusion spray paint in red

Elmer's Painters pen in gold

HERE'S HOW:

1. Tape newspaper on the inside of your mirror so you won't get paint on it when you spray the frame.

2. Place the mirror on newspaper outdoors and spray paint the entire frame gold. Let it dry.

3. Cut the lace to fit the four sides of the frame. Spray the wrong side of the lace with the adhesive and adhere it to the frame, making sure it sticks nicely onto all the curves and crannies.

4. Spray paint over the lace with the red paint. After a few minutes, remove the lace.

5. When the frame is completely dry, run the gold enamel paint marker along the crevices and edges to give it some definition.

6. Hang the mirror and adore yourself.

CHAPTER 11

AWESOME ARTWORK

Have you ever gone to a museum and thought to yourself, **"Wow, I could totally paint that!"** Well, my friend, you should! I mean, if you have 3 million dollars to spend on a Picasso, then put this book down and send me a check. But if you don't, well, **grab a canvas and a few art supplies and make something to liven up your space.** Art is an expression of who we are and what we find beautiful—and it can also cover up a very ugly water heater if placed just right! Trust me on this: Art is the pepper on your eggs, the parsley on your entrée, the cherry on your ice cream. You get the point. So I've come up with some **fun ideas** that might inspire you to make your own art to hang on your own walls. These projects **require very little in the way of time and materials and are super easy to make.** Change them a bit, use different colors, make them even larger than I have—and **you'll be showing in a gallery before you know it.** Remember, all great artists first copied from their teachers. **We all have to start somewhere.**

SEASHELL BUST

Have you ever driven down the road and seen a bunch of plaster sculptures lined up at an outdoor store? I have to admit they can be a bit much. Nonetheless, one day I just broke down and bought a bust that was crying out for embellishment—and this is what happened. Now, it may not be your bag (of shells), but it certainly looks better than it did before. And now I can display it with pride instead of, well, embarrassment!

YOU'LL NEED:

Plaster bust of any size and shape

Newspaper

Lots of seashells

Amazing Goop Household glue

Toothpicks

Tape

Sticky felt for the bottom (optional)

HERE'S HOW:

1. Lay the sculpture on its back on newspaper.

2. Decide where you're going to place your seashells. Glue them onto the bust, two or three at a time, using the toothpicks to dab on the glue instead of globbing it on from the tube. Hold the shells in place with tape until the glue dries.

3. Continue this process until you've glued on all the shells.

4. If you like, place sticky felt on the bottom of the sculpture so it won't scratch your table.

Hint: When working with small objects like shells or pearls, use toothpicks to dab on glue instead of squeezing it from the tube. It's a lot neater that way.

MODERN OFFICE FOLDER ART

I really love making simple art, and I don't care what materials I use to create it. I also like projects that *anyone* can do! With this folder art, there's simply no right or wrong way to make it—and you're not going to believe how easy it is. One more thing: If I can encourage you to create it on office time, all the better! OK, I have an evil streak and now you've seen it. Did I mention that I've gotten in trouble for making office art at almost every job I've ever had? It's been a problem . . .

YOU'LL NEED:

Plastic folders in different colors

Scissors

Large pieces of watercolor paper

Ink pen and ink

Elmer's Glue-All

HERE'S HOW:

1. Cut out 1" to 3" oogly shapes from the folders. They should look like misshapen peanuts and deformed eggs.

2. Play with their positioning on the watercolor paper and get an idea of how they might work together.

3. With the pen and ink, draw squiggly lines in the center of the paper.

4. When the ink is dry, place your oogly shapes over the lines and decide on your composition.

5. Using a small dot of Elmer's in the center of each plastic shape, glue them onto the paper. Let the glue dry.

6. Sign your artwork and put it in a beautiful frame.

SPIN ART

I know that some of you looking at this project are thinking to yourselves, Why in the name of pink tutus did Mark include spin art in his craft book? I'll tell you why: Because I've never had more fun making art than I have with my new spin art machine. Besides, I had a record turntable that I didn't want to throw away. It was screaming to be used in a project, and this worked out well. Just try it and you'll find yourself in the best mood, calmly creating large and small spin art pieces and loving every minute of it. If you don't, I will personally come to your house and give you a foot massage.

You'll need as much paint as you can gather. I used Plaid paints and Krylon spray paints for the larger pieces. For the smaller pieces I used watercolors and various markers. You'll also need a workspace that can get a bit messy, and an old turntable that works but that you don't use anymore.

YOU'LL NEED:

Old record turntable

Screwdriver

Craft knife

Cardboard

Masking or transparent tape

Canvas, cardboard, or watercolor paper of any size and shape that will spin on your record player

Paintbrushes in different sizes

Any kind of paint

Markers, scissors, frame (optional)

HERE'S HOW:

To make a small canvas:

1. First you have to find a way to remove the arm of the turntable to prevent it from getting in the way with a larger canvas. I was able to unscrew mine from its base.

2. Using a craft knife, cut out 5 layers of cardboard the size of a large (33 rpm) record. Tape the layers together in a stack.

3. Make a hole in the exact center of the stack of cardboard to accommodate the spindle (the little nubbin that holds records in place on the turntable).

4. Tape the layers of cardboard to the turntable. They will create enough height so your canvas won't bump into anything on the turntable when it's spinning.

5. With a few loops of tape, attach the back of the canvas to the stack of cardboard, making sure that it will be able to spin freely on the turntable.

6. Plug in the turntable and get it spinning.

7. Dip a brush in the paint or use a marker and touch the canvas; watch the circles form. I like to take the canvas off and stick it down somewhere else so that the center of the canvas is in different places.

Instructions continue on next two pages.

To make a collage:

1. Follow the steps above until you've got a nice collection of work to choose from.

2. Cut the canvases down to different sizes and attach them with tape side by side (like a puzzle) to create your collage.

3. Slap them in a frame. Any color frame will do if you've used as many colors as I have making my spin art.

To make a large canvas:

1. Gather your paints and create a space outdoors where you can work. I used spray paint, house paint, and whatever other paint I had sitting around.

2. Secure the large canvas to the turntable using a generous amount of tape.

3. If you're using spray paint, put plenty of newspaper on your work surface so you don't make a huge mess.

4. Start the spinning and go for it.

PAINT CHIP ART

I will always be the guy who snags way too many paint chips at the hardware store.
I can't help it! They're free and colorful and I just get sticky fingers when I see them all
lined up in perfect order. Oh, well—I feel better now that I've confessed. I have tons of
different projects for these colorful little paper yummies, but this one is by far my favorite.
I hope you like it as much as I do.

YOU'LL NEED:

Lots of paint chips in your
favorite colors

Ruler

Scissors

Piece of sturdy cardboard in a
size you like

Elmer's Glue-All

Frame

HERE'S HOW:

First things first: You're going to spend a bit of time cutting, so
hunker down and put on a good movie or plug in your iPod.

1. Cut the paint chips into 2 ½" x ⅜" strips. You should be able to
   get at least 15 or 16 pieces from each paint chip.

2. Once you've cut up all your chips, put the strips in a bowl and
   get your cardboard ready.

3. Glue the strips on the cardboard like shingles, overlapping
   them as you go. Start at the bottom and work to the top,
   making sure to cover each edge.

4. When you're done with one row, move on to the next, gluing the
   strips until you've covered the entire piece of cardboard.

5. When the glue has dried, slap the artwork in a nice frame and
   you're done.

Note: Because I'm writing a book to inspire, I had my paint chip
art framed professionally to give it some extra panache. They did a
wonderful job and this piece will stay in my home forever now. I do
have to say, though, if you can't afford a good framer, buy a prefab
frame—it will look just as beautiful.

BOOM WALL ART

For this project I raided my nephew's toy box. I have a feeling he won't even notice—I've never seen so much junk in my life! (It's ballet lessons for his birthday from now on.) I started playing around with these toys and all of a sudden, BOOM! I had an idea for a piece of wall art that could also be a place to hang my ever-growing collection of man jewelry. Don't ask. Let's just say my grandmother let me play with her jewelry box when I was young, and even today I like to rummage and try on clip-on earrings. Hey, everyone needs to feel pretty. Don't judge!

YOU'LL NEED:

Drill and very small drill bit

10"-square stretched canvas or piece of ¾"-thick plywood

5 Power Rangers or plastic robots

White acrylic paint

Paintbrush

Ruler

Rebar tie wire or other wire

Wire cutters

E-6000 glue

Comic book, computer images, or your own drawings that say BOOM! or POW! or BLAM!

Elmer's Glue-All

Elmer's Painters pen in blue

HERE'S HOW:

1. Drill five 1"-deep holes on the sides of your canvas or wood.

2. Drill small holes in the back or front of the toys if you need to. Mine had holes all over them so it wasn't necessary.

3. Paint the canvas or wood white and let it dry.

4. While your canvas is drying, cut five 15"-long pieces of wire.

5. Dab E-6000 glue on one end of each piece of wire and push it into a hole in each toy. Let the glue dry.

6. Paste your word images on the canvas with Elmer's and let them dry. You can get images off the Internet or from a comic book or draw your own. You can even just print out the word BOOM! and paste it on. Be creative—it's easy.

7. When your canvas is dry, go over the edges with a blue paint pen to give it some definition.

8. Dab E-6000 glue on the other end of the toy wires and insert them in the holes on the sides of the canvas.

9. Bend the wires so it looks like the toys have just been ejected from the cockpit of a spaceship.

10. Hang the piece on the wall and enjoy it as art—or as a holder for your man jewelry.

BOOM SCULPTURE

Little space guys on wires? Yeah, baby! I'm all for it. I'm still a kid at heart, and creating this little sculpture was a blast. I love the way it wiggles around when I walk by, and my nephews can't stop playing with it. Looks like I may have to make a few more.

YOU'LL NEED:

Small block of wood about 3" high

4"-square piece of wood for the base

Elmer's Wood Glue

Drill with ¼" drill bit

Newspaper

Krylon Fusion spray paint in black (flat)

5 robot/astronaut-type toys (try the 99¢ store)

Spray paint in 4 different colors

Rebar tie wire

Ruler

Wire cutters

E-6000 glue

Elmer's Painters pen in blue

HERE'S HOW:

1. Using wood glue, glue the block of wood to the square piece of wood you've chosen for your base.

2. When the glue is dry, drill a hole in the top center of the wood block.

3. On newspaper outdoors, spray paint the base and one of the action figures black.

4. Spray paint the other four action figures in different colors.

5. Cut five 12" pieces of wire.

6. Glue one end to each of the action figures with E-6000.

7. Glue the other end of the 5 wires into the hole you've drilled in the block of wood.

8. Bend the wires so it looks like the guys are floating around in space.

9. Run the paint pen along the edges of the wood base to give it some dimension. Let it dry.

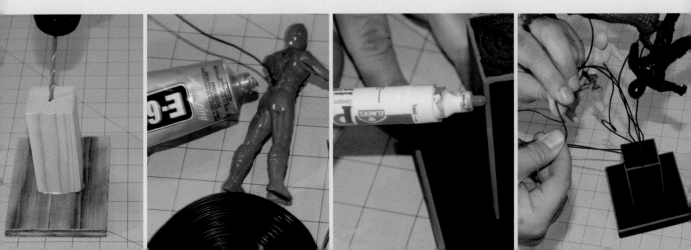

EASY SQUEEZY SQUISH ART

If you want a quick and easy way to make some abstract art in colors that match your home, this is your project. You're basically replacing the cardboard in a nice frame with a second piece of glass and making a see-through picture. You never know how the art will turn out, but the results are always chic and fun. I have a blast making these with my nieces and nephews, though more paint gets on them than on the artwork. Oh, well—it's more fun that way.

I got the colorful frames for this project at IKEA. Not only were they cheap, but they also use plastic instead of glass, so they're much safer to use.

YOU'LL NEED:

Newspaper

2 equal-size picture frames with glass or plastic faces

Different colors of paint

HERE'S HOW:

1. Cover your workspace with newspaper. Remove the glass from the frames and clean each piece carefully.

2. Squeeze or drop the paint like a crazy person all over one of the pieces of glass. Use big globs and small globs and squiggles.

3. Place the second piece of glass on the paint and squish it down. Don't worry if you don't like the result—just toss it in the sink (carefully if it's glass!), wash it off, and start again. It's only paint, right?!

4. Let the art dry for several days lying flat on the newspaper. It's going to take a while to dry since there's so little air between the pieces of glass.

5. Once the piece is dry, place it in the frame and secure it. Hang it on the wall and impress your pals.

CHAPTER 12

INCREDIBLE IKEA IDEAS

I don't know if you've ever been to a friend's home that's filled with **IKEA furniture**. It looks like they've ripped a page out of the catalog and said, "This is what I want!" Don't get me wrong—**I love IKEA**, but I just don't want my house filled with items that literally millions of people have in their homes. If you're anything like me, we're just too special for that. Now, taking an IKEA table or lamp and **sprucing it up**, that's another story, and that's what I've done in this chapter. **IKEA pieces are so basic that for me they're like canvases—clean slates to glue, paint, and misuse in any way I choose.** Benches become table bases, lamps get decoupage treatment, and mirrors are decorated with nailheads! The price is right and you almost can't go wrong if you have a good plan. I guess **my favorite thing to buy at IKEA is the basic square Parsons table**, called the Lack table. It's about 15 bucks and can be stacked, painted, and tortured into anything you want. So **this is a chapter about really thinking outside the box.** Just don't go to IKEA on a Saturday, or you'll never get your project started.

CHINESE JOSS PAPER–COVERED TABLE

Ah, the basic IKEA Lack table. With its clean lines and beautiful flat square top, it's like a canvas just waiting for me to come along and go nuts. I love these tables and I can't get enough of them. This project was inspired by a recent trip to Chinatown, where I stocked up on joss paper, the beautiful Chinese paper that is burned in traditional ceremonies. My Chinese friends are always a bit wary of my using these papers, so my sincere apologies if I've offended anyone.

YOU'LL NEED:

Chinese tea paper or joss paper (check out www.pearlriver.com)

Scissors

IKEA Lack table

Sandpaper or sanding block

Elmer's Glue-All

Cup or plate

1"-wide paintbrush

Old magazine

Minwax Polycrylic Protective Finish

2"-wide paintbrush

HERE'S HOW:

1. Start by cutting off the borders around your joss paper sheets—you won't need them.

2. Lightly sand the table to give texture for the glue to adhere to.

3. Slightly water down the Elmer's glue in a cup or plate so it spreads easily. Just add a few drops at a time until you get a good consistency. You can always add more glue if the mixture gets too runny.

4. Put one sheet of joss paper on a page of an old magazine, spread the glue on the back with the 1" paintbrush, and adhere it to one corner of the table.

5. Add another piece of joss paper next to the first, and continue this process until the entire table is covered, legs and all.

6. When the glue has dried, brush the table with Polycrylic using the 2" brush to give it a nice finish.

7. If you make more than one table, you can put them together to create a long beautiful coffee table for your living room!

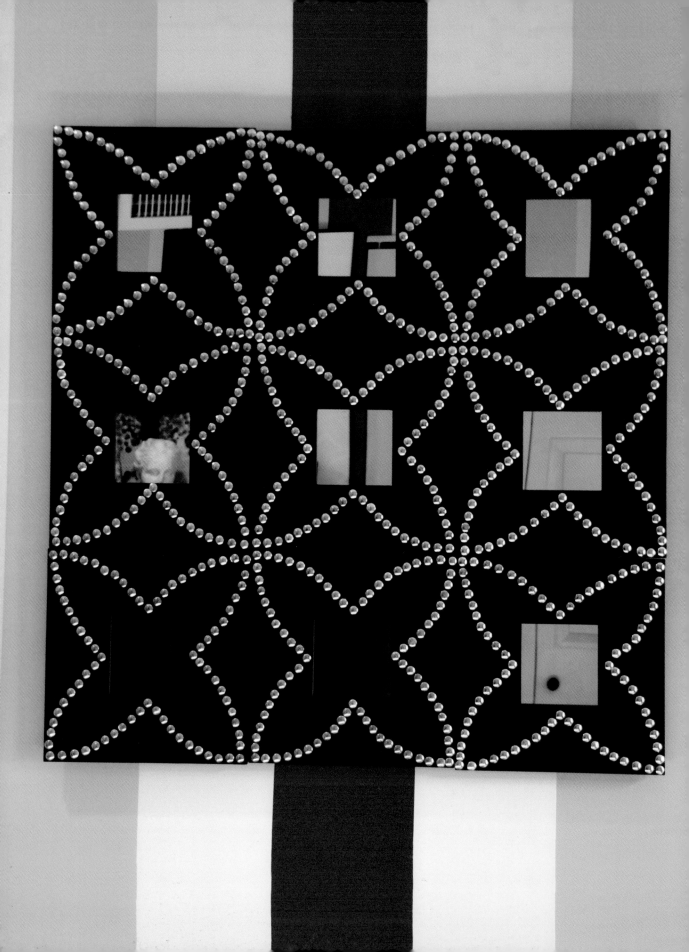

THUMBTACK MALMA MIRRORS

These mirrors are a staple at IKEA and they look terrific clustered together in almost any combination. I decided to take a few boxes of very simple thumbtacks and give the mirrors a nailhead feel. This way, the mirrors take on a masculine look that works in a variety of rooms, from a dining room to a den.

YOU'LL NEED:

9 IKEA Malma mirrors

Pen

Piece of cardboard the same size as the mirror

Scissors

Pencil

800 or so thumbtacks

Needle-nose pliers

Small hammer

HERE'S HOW:

1. Figure out the design you want around your mirrors. Since the mirrors are square, you can make a design on one side of each mirror and repeat it on the other three sides.

2. Draw your design onto the cardboard with a pen to make a template, then cut it out. This will ensure that each mirror has the exact same design.

3. Trace the design onto each mirror frame in pencil (or white pencil if you're using the dark wood Malma mirrors, as I did).

4. Holding a thumbtack with the tip of the pliers, tap it with a hammer on the line you traced around the mirror.

5. Continue this process until you've completed all 9 mirrors.

6. Hang the mirrors either in a big diamond shape or a big square—it's up to you. The mirrors would look great paired with any furniture that also has nailheads.

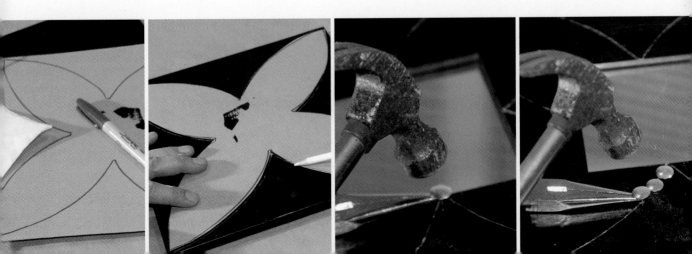

SITTING-ON-A-BRANCH BENCH

This stool is amazing. Not only does it work as a stool, it's also the perfect size for a side table and works great with a large tabletop mounted on it (see page 222). I gave the stool a new life by using simple blue painter's tape to create a design. You can try this technique on a dresser, a closet door—even kitchen cabinets. It's easy to do and looks fantastic.

YOU'LL NEED:

IKEA Benjamin stool in blond wood

1"-wide blue painter's tape

Craft knife

Newspaper

Krylon Fusion spray paint in blue

HERE'S HOW:

1. Using the painter's tape, make a tree trunk on the stool, starting from the bottom corner.

2. Continue by making branches up and across the stool in different sizes and directions, like you would see on a real tree.

3. With the craft knife, taper the ends of the branches to a point. Use the strips of tape you're removing to create smaller branches.

4. When you're done taping, put the stool on newspaper outdoors and spray paint it, inside and out. Use several coats of paint, allowing it to dry at least 10 minutes between coats.

5. When the paint has dried completely, remove the tape to reveal your tree.

CIRCUS TABLES

These IKEA Lack tables look great clustered in a group. And if you enlarge an image enough, you can create an entire scene by putting the tables together like a puzzle. Circus images for a living room, trains or even alphabets for a kid's room—any of these would make for a chic string of tables.

YOU'LL NEED:

Image for enlarging

3 IKEA Lack tables

Scissors

Elmer's Craft Bond Spray Adhesive

Minwax Polycrylic Protective Finish (spray)

Minwax Polycrylic Protective Finish (paintable)

2"-wide latex paintbrush

HERE'S HOW:

1. Enlarge your image to the size of the 3 tables together. (Staples is great for making large photocopies.) It will be printed on several sheets of paper, which you'll have to assemble.

2. Working with the images on a large flat surface (not the IKEA tables yet), remove the excess paper from the edges.

3. Put the three tables in a line, touching. Place the image pieces on the tables and cut them where the tables separate.

4. Starting from the top and working your way down, apply Elmer's spray adhesive on the back of each sheet. Adhere the sheets to the tabletops. Be very careful when you're doing this; once the image is stuck to the table, it's hard to remove.

5. Continue this process until you've covered all 3 tables.

6. Lightly spray the Polycrylic on the tables to protect the image on top. After the first coat has dried, spray several more to give it a nice tough finish, waiting 15 minutes between coats.

7. After the spray adhesive has dried, brush on the liquid Polycrylic with the brush. This way you're sure to have a terrific finish that you can wipe down.

8. Arrange the tables.

Hint: For any projects that call for glued or decoupaged images, make sure they're printed on paper that's at least 24 lbs. Thinner paper just won't work.

GLASS GRÖNÖ LAMPS

Not only are these IKEA Grönö lamps extremely affordable, but they also are the perfect surface for anything you want to put on them. I chose two very dapper gentlemen with canes, but you could use butterflies, bugs, glass chips—you name it! You're limited only by your imagination.

YOU'LL NEED:

Images for copying

Scissors

Pencil

Set of IKEA Grönö lamps

Elmer's Glue-All

1"-wide paintbrush

HERE'S HOW:

1. Enlarge your images to the size of one side of the lamp. I put an image on every side, so I needed four for each lamp.

2. Cut out the images and, with a pencil, trace lightly on the lamp where you'd like to place them.

3. With a small brush, cover the back of the image with Elmer's glue and stick it to the lamp.

4. Glue the remaining images on the other sides of the first lamp, and repeat with the second lamp. Once the glue has dried, add bulbs, plug in your lamps, and see the images glow!

Hint: For any projects that call for glued or decoupaged images, make sure they're printed on paper that's at least 24 lbs. Thinner paper just won't work.

TREETOP TABLETOP

I've said it before and I'll say it again: There's no need to buy new furniture when you can paint or otherwise alter your old furniture to create something special and unique. For this project I used the top of a basic oval oak table that's been sold at IKEA for 25 years. Let's face it: It's U-G-L-Y! With a little tape and paint, however, I've managed to make it into something everyone wants. I even got rid of the base and used a super cool IKEA stool instead, so it's truly one of a kind.

YOU'LL NEED:

Old tabletop

Sandpaper or sanding block

Rag

IKEA Benjamin stool

Elmer's Glue-All

¾"- to 1"-wide blue painter's tape

Craft knife

Newspaper

Krylon spray paint in white

Minwax Polycrylic Protective Finish (optional)

2"-wide paintbrush

HERE'S HOW:

1. Remove the tabletop from the legs and base.

2. Wipe it down with soap and water, then sand it lightly so the table has a "tooth" for the paint to stick to.

3. Wipe the table off with a rag to remove the wood dust.

4. Sand the top of the stool as well to give it some texture and allow the glue to adhere strongly. Wipe it off with a rag to remove dust.

5. Using a generous amount of Elmer's, place the tabletop on the stool and let it dry for a few hours.

6. Use the painter's tape to make a tree trunk on the tabletop, starting from the center of one edge.

7. Continue making branches in different directions and different sizes, just like you would see on a real tree.

8. With your craft knife, taper the ends of the branches to a point.

9. Use the strips you're removing to create smaller branches. Don't worry if you don't like the way it's turning out—you can always move the tape and add or remove branches.

10. When you're done taping, set the table on newspaper outdoors and spray paint it. Give it several coats of paint, allowing it to dry at least 10 minutes between coats.

11. Once the table is dry, remove the tape.

12. *Optional:* To give your tabletop extra protection, coat it with Polycrylic using the brush.

CHAPTER 13

FAB-TASTIC FURNITURE

You may be tempted to skip over this chapter because **these projects look hard, but I assure you they're not.** The wood I used is all standard, and I had to do very little cutting myself. The cutting I did do I actually enjoyed and you will too. Why should you give these projects a try? **Well, have you seen how expensive furniture is these days?** Even the stuff at thrift stores is getting pricy. Plus, it seems like you always have to compromise on size or color or both. I say, take matters into your own hands and **break out the jigsaw and hammer.** I swear you can do this—if I can, you can. Do you really want that awful coffee table just because it's in your price range? Forget it—**for a fraction of the cost you can make something AMAZING!**

TRIPLE-TIER SIDE TABLE

I've always enjoyed making my own furniture. But I'm no professional, so I have to be a bit craftier than a true carpenter would be. I'm fine with my limitations, though. I still enjoy the process and get a kick out of having new furniture in my house that doesn't cost an arm and a leg. So get over the fact that something looks hard and just go for it.

YOU'LL NEED:

Three 24"-diameter tabletops (standard at Lowe's and The Home Depot)

Pencil

Yardstick

Elmer's Wood Glue

Four 3" pieces of 1" x 2" pine

Twenty-four 2" finishing nails

Hammer

Eight 12" pieces of 1" x 2" pine

Sandpaper

Rags

20' of iron-on wood veneer edging

Iron

High-gloss paint in any color

2"-wide latex paintbrush

HERE'S HOW:

1. With a pencil and yardstick, divide each tabletop into 4 equal quarter-circles. Make sure the measurement is precise and marked exactly the same way on each of the tabletops.

2. To make the base, spread a little wood glue on the cut end of each of the four 3" pieces. Attach the legs at the outer edge of one tabletop, where you've drawn your lines. Flip the tabletop over and secure each leg with two finishing nails.

3. Do the same on the middle shelf with four 12" pieces, and on the top shelf with the last four 12" pieces.

4. Spread a generous amount of glue on the bottom of the legs of the middle shelf and glue it to the bottom shelf, matching the position of the other legs. Repeat with the top shelf.

5. Set something heavy on top of the table to create a nice bond between the shelves as the glue dries.

6. Sand the entire table once the glue has dried, and remove the sawdust with a rag.

7. Apply the iron-on veneer around the edge of each tabletop, following the instructions on the package.

8. Paint the table with high-gloss paint, and let it dry completely.

INDIA-INSPIRED BEDSIDE DRESSER

My five-year-old neighbor, Victoria, was mesmerized by this side table, so I guess I know where it will end up after this book is finished. There's nothing better than jewels to liven up an otherwise drab dresser for a girl's room, right? This technique is really simple and can fancy up any plain surface. Try it on mirrors, frames, lamp bases, or drawer pulls (see page 80). If you have plain walls and bedding, your India-inspired furniture can be the focal point of the room.

YOU'LL NEED:

Dresser

Sandpaper and rags (optional)

Newspaper

Krylon Fusion spray paint in purple

Large piece of lace

Elmer's Craft Bond Spray Adhesive

Krylon Metallic spray paint in gold

Faux gems in different colors

Amazing Goop Household glue

Toothpicks

HERE'S HOW:

1. Remove all the hardware from your dresser, sand the surface a little if it's rough, and wipe it clean with a rag.

2. Put the dresser on newspaper outdoors. Spray paint the entire dresser purple. Use several coats of paint, waiting 10 minutes between coats.

3. Spray the lace with the spray adhesive and press it onto the dresser.

4. Lightly spray over the lace with the gold spray paint. Let it dry for a few minutes, then remove the lace.

5. Play with your gems to figure out where you want them; since most lace has a repeat pattern, you could use the pattern as a guide. Glue the gems on with Goop glue, using a toothpick. Then let your creation sparkle!

NAILHEAD DRESSER

From chairs and sofas to mirrors and doors, nailheads have been a staple in home décor forever. Often they're applied one by one by professionals, but at your local fabric store you'll find strips of nailheads that eliminate almost all the work. Pretty soon you'll be embellishing every piece of furniture in your house—I'm sure of it!

YOU'LL NEED:

Plain dresser

Sandpaper (optional)

Rags (optional)

Newspaper (optional)

Krylon Fusion spray paint (high gloss) (optional)

Ruler

Pencil

1 or 2 rolls of nailheads

Wire cutters or heavy-duty scissors

Hammer

Metal file (optional)

HERE'S HOW:

If you're using an unpainted dresser:

1. Remove the dresser drawers and lightly sand them, along with the other pieces of your dresser.

2. Wipe away the excess dust with rags.

3. Put the dresser on newspaper outdoors and paint it. Allow it to dry for at least a day, giving the paint time to cure.

4. Using the ruler and pencil, lightly draw out the design you want to put on the dresser.

5. Unroll the nailhead trim and cut it into lengths that correspond to the lines you've drawn. *Note:* To get a good corner, it's better to connect two pieces of the trim rather than try to bend it at a 90-degree angle.

6. With a hammer, tap in the large tacks that come with your roll of nailheads. Continue until you're done with the entire dresser.

7. Check the corners—some of them may be sharp and will catch on your clothes. Tap in any sharp points with a hammer, or file them down with a metal file. Also, if you nicked your dresser while tapping in the trim, go back and give it a paint touch-up!

If you're using an already painted dresser:

Skip steps 1 to 3 above, and eliminate the sandpaper, rags, newspaper, and spray paint.

STRING PAINT TECHNIQUE DRESSER

I've scoured books, nooks, and crannies for paint techniques that I haven't seen before—with absolutely no luck—so I came up with this one myself. Though I don't knit, I love to buy yarn, and I had to find something to do with it, right? Here's the result, a super-easy technique that you can use on anything from fabric to picture frames. Soon you'll be wrapping and spraying your grandmother! Check out the String Art Pillow on page 40. It uses the same method, except you're wrapping yarn around fabric instead of furniture.

YOU'LL NEED:

Dresser that needs some lovin'

Newspaper

Krylon Fusion spray paint in 2 different colors (I used Honeydew for the undercoat and River Rock for the top coat)

Skein of yarn

Rebar wire drawer handles (page 82)

HERE'S HOW:

1. Put the dresser on newspaper outdoors. Spray the dresser with the lighter color of paint. Let it dry for at least 1 hour.

2. Remove one of the drawers, tightly wrap the yarn around it in a random pattern, and tie a knot with the yarn at the back of the drawer, where it will not be sprayed.

3. Lightly spray with the second paint color. Let it dry for about 10 minutes, then carefully remove the string.

4. Repeat this process with the other drawers, and with the top and sides of the dresser.

5. Add the rebar wire drawer handles (page 82).

SUPER SIMPLE SHELVING

Although you need a lot of different wood pieces for this project, your local lumber or hardware store will cut them to size for you. The shelf is made of standard-size pieces of wood, so all you have to do is go home and assemble it. Not bad when you think about it, right? It's certainly much better than paying all that extra money to have something everyone else has.

YOU'LL NEED:

1" x 8" pine plank cut into:

• One 22" piece

• One 20 ½" piece

• Two 7 ¼" pieces

• Two 6 ½" pieces

Elmer's Wood Glue

20 or so finishing nails

Hammer

Pencil

Drill with ¼" drill bit

Sand

Minwax Wood Stain

HERE'S HOW:

1. Lay the 22" piece flat.

2. Squirt some wood glue on one edge of the 20 ½" piece of wood and center it on top of the 22" piece of wood at the edge. Hammer in three finishing nails after the glue sets.

3. Glue one 7 ¼" piece on each side of the two pieces you just put together. You'll see how they fit perfectly on each side. Nail them in place.

4. Set the 6 ½" pieces on top. Apply wood glue where they touch and then nail them in with finishing nails.

5. Drill two holes in the back about 2" down from the top of the shelf and about 16" apart so you can hang your shelf.

6. Sand the shelf and then stain it in a color you like.

Remember: You can have all the pieces of wood for this project cut for you at your local lumber or hardware store.

PAGODA ÉTAGÈRE

After seeing shelves like these at high-end furniture stores for way too much money, I decided to whip up an étagère myself in a shape I've always loved—a pagoda. This is made with standard pieces of wood, and all you have to do is visit your local hardware store and give them the wood list I've provided. After that, it's a bit of nailing and staining—and then finding the perfect place to put your shelves.

YOU'LL NEED:

Elmer's Wood Glue

1 box of 2 ¼" finishing nails

Hammer

Pencil

Sandpaper

Rag

Newspaper

Krylon Fusion spray paint in red (high gloss)

WOOD LIST:

Sixteen 15"-long 2x2s

Four 4"-long 2x2s

½"-thick birch plywood cut into:

• One 10" square

• One 12 ½" square

• One 15" square

• One 16 ½" square

• One 19" square

HERE'S HOW:

1. With wood glue, attach four of the 15"-long legs to the 10" square of birch, then nail them in using two nails per leg.

2. Repeat this process with the 12 ½" square, the 15" square, and the 16 ½" square.

3. Nail the 4" (2x2) legs to the 19" square; this is the bottom shelf.

4. Once all the legs are on, stack your shelves from largest to smallest and center them so they make a perfect pagoda.

5. Mark the leg positions lightly with a pencil, remove the top three shelves, and wood glue the bottom two together.

6. Continue gluing the shelves until you reach the top. Place something heavy on one of the upper shelves to help the glue set.

7. When your shelves are dry, sand the structure down to remove all the rough edges. Use a rag to dust it off.

8. Set the shelves on newspaper outdoors, and spray paint.

9. When the paint is dry, add your knickknacks!

Remember: You can have all the pieces of wood for this project cut for you at your local lumber or hardware store.

CUSTOMIZED OUTDOOR UMBRELLA

I was tired of heading to the hardware store every time I needed an umbrella for my backyard. Instead, I decided to take matters into my own hands and make an umbrella. This project was much easier than I thought it would be, and you'll have no trouble with it as long as you have some basic sewing skills. But it will take some time, so be patient! Once you make your first one, you'll be making tons of different ones to match your house.

Most umbrellas are separated into six different fabric triangles of equal shape and size. With some umbrellas, these triangles go all the way to the tip of the umbrella and meet. With others, there's a hole in the top center and a circle of fabric that goes around the hole to keep out the rain. Mine is the kind with the circle at the top.

YOU'LL NEED:

Old umbrella in a stand (and the old fabric)

3 yards (for solid colors) or 6 yards (for stripes) of heavy-duty (or outdoor) fabric

Scissors

Straight pins

Sewing machine and thread

8 yards of fringe (optional)

¼ yard of Ultrasuede or heavy-duty fabric that will not fray (such as vinyl)

HERE'S HOW:

1. Remove the old fabric from your umbrella.

2. Use one of the triangular pieces of fabric to make a pattern, adding ½" seam allowance all the way around. If you also have a circle of fabric at the top, make a pattern for that and add a ½" seam allowance all the way around.

3. Lay the pattern on your new fabric and cut out the number of shapes you need.

4. Hem the pieces at the edge (the widest part of the triangle) by folding up ½" and stitching in a straight line. Hem the circle as well if you have one.

5. Lay your pieces together side by side, pin, and sew right sides together using ½" seam allowance. Use the old umbrella as your guide. It's really easy, I assure you.

6. If you're adding fringe, sew it around the umbrella and around the edge of the circle if you have one.

7. Cut the Ultrasuede into small pocket shapes (like a shirt pocket, but smaller) and sew them on the underside of each seam of the umbrella to hold the tip of each rib (the arms that extend from the center).

8. Stretch the fabric over the ribs. If you have a fabric circle, put it right on top. The circle is usually held in place with a screw-on ball, but if you don't have that, just use a small nail.

CHAPTER 14

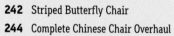

SENSATIONAL SEATING

When my friend Tilda was pregnant she was stuck in bed for two months before her gorgeous baby was born. **We sat there together and ate and ate and ate.** If you had seen how much my butt grew, you would have thought I was the pregnant one. Well, a similar thing happened while **writing this book**. I sat down and wrote and ate and wrote and ate. **Fortunately I was able to sit on a few very chic chairs while I was writing**—the very same seats you'll see in this chapter. These chairs, ottomans, and benches are **much better in sets of two** and three, but I made only one each for the purposes of this book. Can you imagine an entire dining room set of the Striped Butterfly Chairs around a white circular table? I certainly can. What about four square ottomans smooshed together to make an **incredible coffee table**? Slap a big tray on it and you're all set. The point is, **if you're going to be on your butt, do it in style**. Don't you and your bum deserve to be sitting on something **spectacular**?

STRIPED BUTTERFLY CHAIR

I like my Umbra Oh! Chair very much, but I always wish it had a bit more pizazz. After a few failed attempts, I came up with this idea to give it a pop art feel. I like this pattern so much I'm thinking about re-creating it on a wall somewhere in my house. If you're not a butterfly person, why not try it with stripes and, say, images of skulls or cupcakes? Whichever way you go, I hope this project inspires you to give your basic chairs some zing.

YOU'LL NEED:

Umbra Oh! Chair (available at The Container Store)

Newspaper

Blue painter's tape

Krylon Fusion spray paint in black

Images of butterflies copied onto different bright-colored paper

Scissors

Elmer's Glue-All

1"-wide paintbrush

Minwax Polycrylic Protective Finish

HERE'S HOW:

1. Set the chair on newspaper outdoors. Tape stripes on the chair with the blue tape. Mine were about 1 ½" wide.

2. Spray paint the entire chair with the black paint and let it dry.

3. Remove the tape and your chair will be striped.

4. Cut out the butterfly images and play around with them on the chair so you get the positioning just right.

5. Paint the back of the images with Elmer's glue and stick them to the chair in place.

6. Once all the butterflies are glued on and dry, paint over the entire chair with several coats of Polycrylic, waiting about 30 minutes between coats. Let the chair dry overnight.

7. Now you're ready to put your bum in something even cooler than bellbottoms!

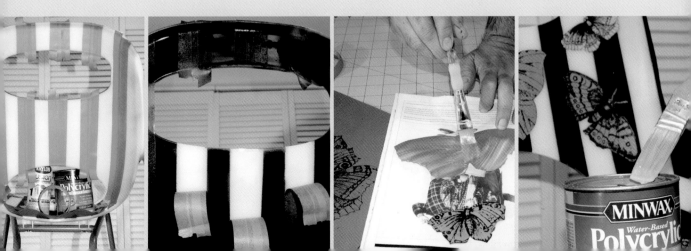

COMPLETE CHINESE CHAIR OVERHAUL

Everything is a canvas to me, even things I find on the street. I just could not bear to leave this chair to be picked up for landfill—it would have been way too sad. Instead I gave it my heart and soul, and now it has a permanent place in my home. I love it just as much as I love my other furniture. Think twice before you toss out something. Give it a little TLC, and you'll be able to enjoy it all over again. I promise.

YOU'LL NEED:

Upholstered wood chair in need of some love

Newspaper

Screwdriver

Sandpaper

Rags

Krylon Fusion spray paint in red

Black-and-white images (check out Dover books for great clip art)

Scissors

Elmer's Glue-All

1"-wide paintbrush

Minwax Polycrylic Protective Finish

2"-wide latex paintbrush

Ruler

White pencil

1 yard of black fabric

12 yards of white ¼"-wide ribbon

Sewing machine and thread

Enough 2"-thick foam to cover the seat; foam cutter; marker (optional); glue gun and glue sticks

Staple gun

HERE'S HOW:

1. On newspaper outdoors, flip the chair upside down and remove the foam cushion.

2. Lightly sand the entire chair. Wipe off the dust with a rag.

3. Spray paint the entire chair red. Give it several coats, waiting at least 10 minutes between coats.

4. Cut out your images, paying careful attention to the details.

5. With the 1"-wide brush, paint Elmer's glue on the back of the images and attach them to the chair.

6. When all the images are dry, give the chair a coat of the Polycrylic using the wider brush.

7. Let dry and coat again if needed.

8. Draw lines 2½" apart in a grid pattern on the black fabric using a white pencil.

9. Sew the ribbon over each line of the grid to create the seat fabric.

10. Rip off the old fabric (and the foam too, if you like) from the old seat cushion.

11. *Optional:* If you're using new foam, trace the wood shape with a marker on the foam and cut it with a foam cutter or serrated bread knife. Hot glue the new foam to the wood seat.

12. Stretch the fabric over the seat and staple it all around the underside of the seat.

13. Flip the chair upside down (do it on your bed so you don't scratch it) and screw on the new seat cushion.

VINYL APPLIQUÉ CHAIR AND OTTOMAN

My dad did upholstery on the side when I was growing up. I was lucky enough to have a variety of wonderful scraps of faux leather to play with and a dad who encouraged me to do so. I've been experimenting a lot lately with gluing vinyl on things, and this chair and ottoman worked out quite beautifully. I think even my dad would enjoy it.

YOU'LL NEED:

1 yard each of vinyl in 3 different colors

Scissors

2 tubes of Amazing Goop Household glue

Chair and ottoman in need of a face-lift

HERE'S HOW:

To make the chair:

1. Cut the vinyl into pieces 1 ½" x 2". The rectangles don't have to be perfect, nor do they have to be this exact size; they can vary a little here and there.

2. When you've cut a large amount, start gluing pieces one by one on the edge of the chair with the Goop glue. Overlap them just a bit when you're placing them side by side.

3. Once you've completed the edge, repeat the process with the next row, above the first, overlapping the pieces side by side and from row to row as well.

4. Continue until you've completed the entire chair.

To make the ottoman:

1. Start on the bottom of the ottoman, gluing the first row of vinyl all the way around and overlapping side by side.

2. Continue with the next row, overlapping side by side as well as from row to row.

3. When you get to the top of the ottoman, start at the edge and glue the vinyl completely around the shape.

4. Continue inward until you get to the center.

5. Cut out a circle or small square and glue it to the center to finish it off.

HAND-PAINTED CATALOG SLIPCOVER

We've all got one—the ugly basement couch that's too good to toss out but too ugly to properly decorate around. Even the most talented sewers might not want to take the time to make an entire slipcover, and between that and the money you'd have to spend, you might as well buy a new sofa.

But I have a better solution! You can buy a neutral slipcover that, as far as I'm concerned, would be the *perfect* canvas for making your own special sofa. (Sure Fit makes neutral canvas slipcovers at a fair price.) With a little house paint left over from your living room, you can have a matching sofa in no time. I can hear it already: I can't paint like that, I'll mess it up! Guess what? You can do it! It's easy as long as you follow my directions and take a few simple steps to prepare yourself. To begin, put your sofa on a large dropcloth in an area where you can paint all around it. As I said, you're turning your slipcover into a canvas. If a little bit of paint seeps through to the sofa underneath, who cares? You're covering it up anyway.

YOU'LL NEED:

Sofa

Dropcloth

Iron and ironing board

Pre-made slipcover

20 large safety pins

White chalk pencil

2 yards of scrap fabric for practice

Paint

Paintbrushes

Large piece of cardboard

HERE'S HOW:

1. Set your sofa on a large dropcloth. Iron the slipcover so you have a nice flat fabric to work with.

2. Place the slipcover on the sofa and get it just right. Use the safety pins to keep it in place perfectly if you need to.

3. Lightly draw flowers (or stripes) on the scrap fabric. Practice painting on the scrap fabric before you tackle the slipcover.

4. Once you have that process down, lightly draw your pattern on the back, front, and sides of the slipcover.

5. Paint the back of the sofa first so you can get in even more practice before you start on the front. Paint one section at a time until you've covered the entire sofa.

6. Remove the slipcover from the sofa when all the paint is dry and place it on the cardboard on a large table.

7. Continue painting the pattern in the areas that were tucked into the sides and back of the sofa. This will ensure that your sofa looks great even if the cover slips a little.

For these projects I used Benjamin Moore flat paints in Chocolate Brown for the flower sofa and Jalapeno Pepper, Twilight Gold, Honey Wheat, and Tropicana Cabana for the striped sofa.

UPHOLSTERED PLEATHER OTTOMAN

You see them everywhere, and chances are you have one or two, like I do. I'm talking about those square pleather-covered ottomans that you can grab for about 25 bucks at any major chain store. Now, as much as I love them, I'll be darned if my pleather ottoman is going to look like everyone else's. So I came up with this easy project. Even with the most basic sewing skills, you'll be able to do this in a snap and have your house looking like a *Home and Garden* photo spread in no time. You'll have some left-over fabric that you can easily use for matching pillows.

YOU'LL NEED:

Ottoman

Screwdriver

2 yards of 60"-wide fabric

Straight pins

Sewing machine and thread

Staple gun

HERE'S HOW:

1. Take off the bottom panel of the ottoman (the wood base with the legs).

2. Place the ottoman flat on a table and cover it with the fabric, with the good side against the ottoman. Make sure it's even on all sides. You'll have excess hanging over the edge, which you'll need.

3. Pin straight lines starting at each corner of the ottoman and going down each edge, keeping the fabric even all the way around. Check that you have a snug fit.

4. Once you've pinned all four edges and you have a good fit, cut off the excess fabric about 1" away from the pins.

5. Remove the cover and take it to the sewing machine.

6. Sew straight lines where you placed the pins and continue all the way down to the edges of the fabric where you were not able to pin.

7. Turn the cover right side out, poke out the corners, and slip it over the ottoman to make sure it fits well. Adjust if necessary.

8. Turn the ottoman over and staple the extra fabric all the way around the base, pulling it tight to make the top smooth.

9. Replace the bottom panel of the ottoman, and put your feet up!

ROUND SLIPCOVERED GRANNY OTTOMAN

I define "Granny Chic" as anything in your world that looks like your granny made it or bought it. Maybe it's a scarf, a sweater, eyeglasses, or, in my case, an ottoman. Some may like the "Granny Chic" style I used for this particular ottoman, and others may not. For those who don't, here's what my granny used to say: "If you don't have anything nice to say, make sure you're close enough so I can jab you with my knitting needle."

YOU'LL NEED:

Circular ottoman

Tape measure

2 yards of heavy-duty fabric

Scissors

Sewing machine and thread

Iron and ironing board

Pencil

Straight pins

Hot glue gun and glue sticks

5 yards of 1"-wide ribbon

Enough fringe to circle the base of the ottoman

HERE'S HOW:

1. Measure the height and circumference of your ottoman. (Mine was 17" high by 60" around.)

2. Add 1" to each measurement to give you the ½" seam allowance you'll need when you sew your cover. (For my ottoman, the measurement was 18" x 61".) Use this measurement to cut a rectangle from the fabric.

3. With right sides together, using ½" seam allowance, stitch the small sides (in my case, the 18" sides) of the rectangle together. This will create a big tube. Iron the seam open.

4. Place the ottoman upside down on the back of the remaining fabric and trace around it lightly with a pencil.

5. Add ½" all the way around what you've just traced and cut it out. This is the top part of the ottoman slipcover.

6. Fold the fabric circle in half and then half again (so it looks like a quarter of a pie); then mark the north, south, east, and west points of the circle with a pencil.

7. Mark four equal parts on one end of your fabric tube by folding it in half and then half again.

8. With right sides together (the tube is inside out), match the north, south, east, and west marks on the circle to the four marks on the tube and pin together.

9. Place pins between each of the four pins you've just placed.

10. Using ½" seam allowance, sew around the circle, carefully removing the pins as you go along.

Instructions continue on next two pages.

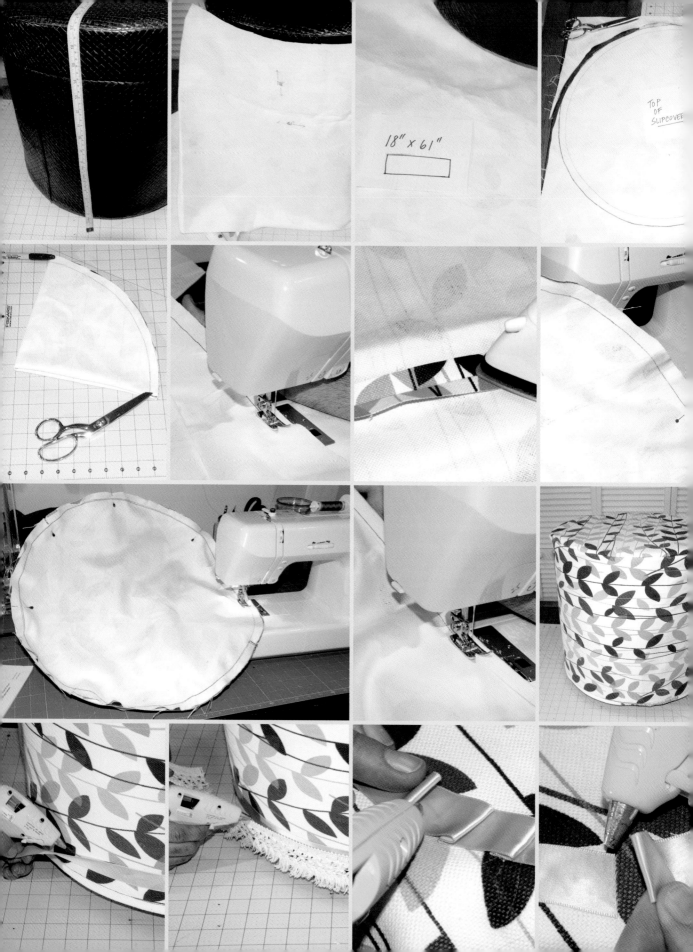

11. Fold up the open part of the tube ½" and hem the slipcover.

12. Place the slipcover on the ottoman. Use the glue gun to attach half of the ribbon around the base of the ottoman, high enough so it will peek above the top of the fringe, which you'll add next.

13. Hot glue the fringe around the base of the ottoman.

14. Glue the rest of the ribbon around the top edge of the ottoman, making little folds every 1 ½" all the way around. This creates a nice pleated and tucked effect.

15. When you reach the end of the circle, simply fold the ribbon under and attach it with a tiny dot of glue.

MUMMY CHAIR

This was absolutely the easiest possible way I could give a chair a face-lift without driving myself nuts. I like everything about it, including the fact that when I'm tired of it, I can rip off the striped fabric and make myself a super-duper-long multicolor scarf. This is also a great way to make a few mismatched chairs into a matching set in no time.

YOU'LL NEED:

4 yards of knit fabric in a print you like

Scissors

Hot glue gun and glue sticks

Chair in need of a face-lift

HERE'S HOW:

1. Lay out your fabric and cut 5"-wide strips in 4-yard lengths.

2. Starting at the bottom of one leg, begin to wrap a strip of fabric as you would apply an Ace bandage to a sprained ankle.

3. Work your way up the leg, wrapping the fabric so you don't see any wood. Once you've completed a leg, start on the rest of the chair.

4. Hot glue the edge of the first wrapped strip to a new strip and keep going until you've covered the entire chair.

5. Once the wrapping is done, you might want to secure some of the knit strips by dabbing on a little glue to keep them together or in place.

Hint: You need to cut this knit fabric in strips the entire length of your yardage. Knit fabric tends to roll at the edges, so you want to cut it only this way and not in strips the width of the fabric.

TEMPLATES

For a number of projects in this book, you'll need templates to trace onto wood, metal, contact paper, fabric, and so on. I encourage you to use your creativity and come up with an image or design of your own—I know you can do it! But if you don't have something specific in mind, feel free to use what I've drawn below. You can photocopy the template and enlarge it to size (the suggested percentage is given for each one), or you can just use it as a guide for your own drawing. Either way, cut out the design and trace around it to achieve the look you want. The important thing is to have fun and make every project your own unique creation!

BIRDCAGE PILLOW, page 42
**BIRD-ON-A-BRANCH
DINNER NAPKINS,** page 88
Birds
Enlarge 200 percent

**MOROCCAN-INSPIRED
STAINED GLASS WINDOW,** page 54
Moroccan tile
Enlarge 175 percent

HAND-STITCHED CURTAIN PANEL, page 60
Bird
Enlarge 200 percent

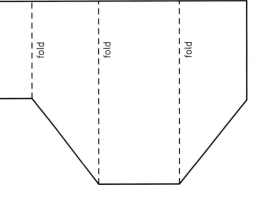

fold   fold   fold   fold

CERAMIC BIRDHOUSE CANDELABRA, page 102
Birdhouse chimney
Enlarge 125 percent

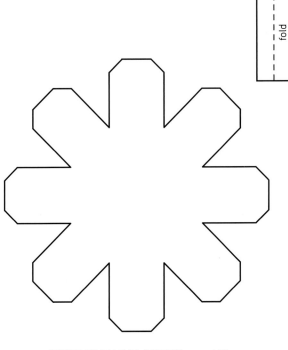

SILVER TRAY WALL SCONCE, page 100
Candle holder
Enlarge 135 percent

MOROCCAN SIDE TABLE, page 114
Moroccan arch
Enlarge 325 percent

**TAPPED-ALUMINUM
WALL SCONCE**, page 154
Large leaf
Medium leaf
Small leaf
Center piece
Enlarge each template 200 percent

A

B

C

E

F

D

**BLOCK-PRINTED
SUZANI BLANKET,** page 172
Stamp A
Stamp B
Stamp C
Stamp D
Stamp E
Stamp F
Enlarge each template 175 percent

TONY DUQUETTE–INSPIRED MIRROR, page 184
Fleur-de-lis
Enlarge 400 percent

STUFF I LIKE TO HAVE AROUND THE HOUSE

All your projects will be easier and more economical if you have the right tools and materials to begin with. A lot of the items in this list (like screwdrivers) are things everyone should have around the house. Others (like faux flowers) are more for us crafty types. Either way, you'll be glad you have them on hand.

ALUMINUM FLASHING This comes in squares or in a roll in different widths. It's great for projects that require metal because it's easy to cut and holds its shape when bent. Also, it doesn't rust!

AMAZING GOOP HOUSEHOLD GLUE AND E-6000 These are the best glues to use on anything and everything. Smooth it out with an ice cube to get it perfect! Try it, you'll see.

BOOKS, OLD You can use the pages to make vintage-looking matting for artwork or photos, to cover lamp bases, or to decorate your walls; the covers are great for boxes and lots of other art projects.

BUCKETS You'll need big buckets for mixing plaster of Paris and for keeping water and sponges nearby while you work.

BUTTONS Beginning today, start collecting buttons! They're decorative and you can glue them on frames, lampshades, mirrors—you name it. My favorite place to buy buttons is the 99¢ store.

CLAMPS When you're gluing things together, small metal clamps will help keep things in place while they dry. Plastic clothespins can serve the same purpose—and for even less money! You can get them at the 99¢ store.

CLEAR LATEX I use clear water-based latex to coat and protect tons of projects. Minwax Polycrylic Protective Finish is the best; stick with that brand for all your finishing needs, and you'll see what I mean.

CONTAINERS, RECYCLED C'mon, how often do you need a place to store pencils, old brushes, and tools? Don't buy a new container—use what you have around the house.

CRAFT KNIVES These are the perfect tools for making clean cuts. I use Olfa and X-Acto knives, but you can usually get a package of decent box cutters at the 99¢ store, so give those a try, too. I go through so many of these that I always have several around as a backup.

CUTTING MAT This is a piece of flexible plastic that you can use your craft knife on over and over again without harming it. It's perfect for precise cutting and also has a 1"-square grid for easy measuring.

DRILL AND DRILL BITS Get a nice, sturdy drill and a good selection of drill bits, If you take good care of them, they'll last forever. Stay away from cheap tools—they just don't last!

ELMER'S GLUE-ALL The basic white stuff is great for all craft projects, especially decoupage.

ELMER'S WOOD GLUE For small wood projects where it's almost impossible to get a tiny nail in place, this stuff will really hold your work together. You can also use it to secure pieces of wood until you can hammer in a nail. And to stabilize wobbly old pieces of furniture, just fill in the cracks with wood glue. You'll see what a difference it makes!

EXTENSION CORDS Let's just say that sometimes your glue gun does not quite reach your worktable.

FABRIC SCRAPS Keep scraps from your sewing projects or old clothes. You never know when they'll come in handy for decorating a lamp, wrapping a chair, or making fabric door beads.

FAUX FLOWERS AND LEAVES Spruce up a lampshade, decorate a frame, and have extras around—you never know when you might need them.

FELT A great material for graphic fabric projects, like pillows and curtains, that doesn't fray at the edges.

GLITTER GLUE Glitter glue will add sparkle to any project. I never leave the house without some in my backpack! Michaels arts and crafts stores have a great selection.

GLUE STICKS What would we do without them? They're a nice clean way to use glue.

GOGGLES   It doesn't matter if you're drilling or sawing or hammering for just one second. You need to protect your eyes!

HAMMER   A must for every toolbox. I recommend having several sizes on hand: a large one for building furniture and a smaller one for more detailed projects.

HOT GLUE GUN   Though I'm not a huge fan of the hot glue gun, it really works well for keeping something in place while you work with another adhesive. I think it's actually best for gluing fabrics together.

JIGSAW   Made especially for cutting curves, a jigsaw with a variety of blades will serve you well in all kinds of craft projects. My Skil jigsaw with a scroll blade works like a charm.

LAMINATING MACHINE   If you like to make laminated projects (like the wall sconce in this book) and you can afford a laminator, you should get one. It's a blast to have around the house!

LEVEL   This is a must in any home and for so many craft projects, from making tables to hanging pictures. Get a small level that's no more than 12" long. You can pick one up almost anywhere these days.

METALLIC SPRAY PAINTS   What looks better sprayed silver or gold? When it comes to crafts, everything! Krylon makes the best metallic paints around.

NEEDLE-NOSE PLIERS   Super for picking up tiny things and bending small wire.

NEWSPAPERS   You need these to keep your work area clean when you're painting or spray painting, and to protect parts of projects that aren't being painted.

NIGHTLIGHT, PLUG-IN   One of the easiest ways to light a project is to plug in a nightlight to the end of an extension cord. It's safe and gives off a very nice low-wattage glow.

OOKS   What's an OOK, you ask? Made by a company called OOK, these are self-leveling sawtooth hangers that will help you hang all sorts of projects, from mirrors to artwork.

PAINTBRUSHES   Find them anywhere, from the 99¢ store to fine art stores, and make sure you take care of them. It's good to have brushes in a number of different widths; for craft projects 1" and 2" widths are best.

PAINT CHIPS   You can pick up free samples at any store that sells paint. Paint chips allow you to see what colors work well together, plus you can use them to make some really neat art projects!

PAINT THINNER   This stuff is flammable, so be careful with it. It's great for getting rid of all kinds of messes and can even remove gooey glue. Just dab a bit on a cotton swab to use.

PAPER CLIPS   These can substitute for a wire hook in a pinch. Just unfold the clip and bend it into the shape you need.

PAPER CUTTER   Perfect for making straight edges and long cuts, getting that perfectly square edge, and cutting several sheets of paper at once.

PAPER GROCERY BAGS   These are really useful to hold glass or mirror pieces while you're breaking them up with a hammer.

PAPER TOWELS AND RAGS   You need an arsenal of clean-up supplies at your disposal. You can cut up old T-shirts and keep them around for cleaning up all the great messes you'll make when crafting.

PENCILS   Have these on hand at all times. You'll need them for sketching, tracing, outlining, and marking measurements.

PERMANENT MARKERS   Sharpie is a popular brand of permanent markers that write on most any surface. They're great on metal, where other markers may not work.

PINKING SHEARS I love these shears with notched blades, which are made for finishing cloth edges with a zigzag cut for decoration or to prevent unraveling or fraying. I have one pair for paper and one pair for fabrics.

PINS, BALL POINT These will help you hold two pieces of fabric in place for sewing, and other tiny things in place while you work.

PLASTER OF PARIS Experiment and have fun with this stuff. You can use it to embellish frames and mirrors, make plaster sculptures, cast candleholders, and lots more.

POPSICLE STICKS, CHOPSTICKS, AND WOODEN COFFEE STIRRERS Use these and lots of Elmer's Wood Glue to make planter boxes, sculptures, frames—even to decorate a table.

Q-TIPS Perfect for dabbing on small bits of glue or taking up a little drip of paint while you work.

RIBBON Faille and satin ribbon adds a nice decorative touch to so many projects: finishing the edges of curtains, lampshades, or ottomans; sewing onto pillows; hanging picture frames the old-fashioned way. So don't throw away those ribbon pieces—save them for a crafty day!

RULERS Everybody needs rulers to use as straight edges as well as to measure things. It's best to have a metal ruler to make cuts with your craft knives.

SANDPAPER AND SANDING SPONGES Aside from sandpaper's obvious purpose—to smooth rough edges—it's also perfect for giving texture to smooth items before you add glue or paint to them. The rough surface gives the glue or paint something to stick to.

SCISSORS FOR PAPER AND FABRIC Invest in a pair of fabric scissors (and don't use them for anything else!). I like Fiskars, but there are other brands out there. For paper, it's good to have several pairs of scissors so you don't have to waste your time sharpening. Try the 99¢ store for a decent pair.

SCISSORS, DECORATIVE You can get these at Michaels arts and crafts stores in lots of different shapes—and you'll want them all. Use them to give your paper projects beautiful borders, from antique photo edges to wild zigzag edges.

SCREWDRIVERS No home should be without a basic set of screwdrivers, both regular and Phillips head. You can paint the tops of the Phillips screwdrivers one color so you can easily identify them in your tool can.

SCREWS AND NAILS Small and big, long and short, fat and thin, wood and metal—they will always be useful.

SCRUBBERS You know how messy you can be, so make sure to have both small and large ones on hand.

SEWING MACHINE Indispensable! My Kenmore travels with me wherever I go.

SHADOW-BOX FRAMES These are a wonderful alternative to regular frames. They give dimension to anything you put in them, even flat items. Get a bunch in different sizes. They look amazing resting on a shelf, or you can hang them. Many come with Velcro and a fuzzy back so you can mount them just about anywhere.

SNAP-IN SOCKET-AND-CORD SET WITH SWITCH These are great for all your lamp projects. They use a candelabra-based bulb (the smaller bulbs), are safe to use, and don't need wiring.

SPRAY ADHESIVE This type of spray glue leaves a nice even coat on your projects. There are strong- and light-tack adhesives, and the light-tack ones allow you to reposition your work until it dries—very helpful when you're decoupaging images. Both Elmer's and Krylon make good adhesives.

SPRAY WATER BOTTLE Next time you finish a bottle of glass cleaner, save it and fill it with water for your workroom. Spraying water on projects that use paint can produce wonderful effects. It can cloud ink and make spray paint gather and dry in terrific patterns.

STAPLE GUN, HEAVY-DUTY The JT21 is great for small upholstery projects, and the staples are easy to pull out if you make a mistake.

STAPLER The simple stapler is not just for attaching papers to each other. You'd be surprised how often I use this crafty little tool for my projects.

STICKY BACK FOAM Kids have always known how fun this stuff is. I like to use it for making stamps that I dip in paint to decorate walls, curtains, and lots of other things.

STICKY FELT Sticky felt is perfect to put on the underside of projects to protect your tabletops. You can also use it for appliqués, so you don't have to apply pins before you sew.

TAPE Blue painter's tape, masking tape, transparent tape—you need them all! Have plenty around for your projects.

TAPE MEASURE No home should be without one, especially when you're working on large-scale projects like wall treatments.

TIN SHEARS With all the beautiful projects in this book that call for flexible metal, you'll want to have a nice pair of tin shears. These make cuts with a serrated blade so the metal edges aren't sharp.

TOMATO CAGES Need a structure to make that fancy lamp or candelabra? A tomato cage is a great place to start. They come in lots of sizes and they're quite inexpensive.

TOOTHPICKS When applying glue to small objects like glass beads, it's much easier—and neater—to use toothpicks rather than squeeze the whole tube.

TURPENTINE You need this to clean the brushes whenever you're working with oil-based paint.

TWINE From tying up your recycled newspapers to wrapping a lampshade, twine is your friend. And it now comes in fantastic colors, so stock up!

WIRE, SMALL GAUGE, AND REBAR TIE You'll want to have wire around for everyday use and for craft use. In this book there are lamps, candelabras, and drawer handles that are made mostly, or completely, of wire.

WIRE CUTTERS Get a pair with spring action. They're easy to work with and give you more control on your projects.

WOOD FILLER This stuff comes in a tube and can be used for cracks, nail holes, and gouges in all kinds of wood.

WOOD SCRAPS Keep a variety of shapes and sizes. They're useful for all kinds of things.

WORK GLOVES Get a pair in cotton and one in leather, and make sure they fit well so you can really use your fingers.

RESOURCE GUIDE

These are the fantastic companies, products, and resources I've used for this book. Because of my work, I get to try many different products. After years of experimenting, I've found that these companies make terrific products with consistently good results. I assure you that you'll feel that same after using their products.

99¢ STORES, DOLLAR TREE

What a great resource for just about anything you might need. Glass plates, candles, toothpicks, Popsicle sticks—you name it. You can't assume that everything will be in stock, but more often than not you'll find at least a piece of your crafting puzzle there for only a buck.

AMAZING GOOP HOUSEHOLD GLUE AND E-6000
www.eclecticproducts.com

On my worktable there is always a tube of Amazing Goop Household glue or E-6000 squeezed to death. I use this glue for almost every project I make and you too must have it in your craft kit. When I say this will hold anything, I mean it! I have not found a better glue on the market. If you want your craft projects to last, put them together with Goop or E-6000.

ART-O-GRAPH
www.artograph.com

This company makes some amazing tools that will help your crafting go smoothly, such as light boxes for tracing and machines that project an image on a wall so you can trace it in various sizes. I'm in love with my light box, and my basic Tracer projector has helped me with countless wonderful art projects!

BENJAMIN MOORE PAINTS
www.benjaminmoore.com

I will not paint a room with anything but Benjamin Moore. It's just that simple! The paint's quality, the range of colors, and the way it covers are just wonderful. Natura, their fantastic new line of eco-friendly paint, is much better for the environment than traditional paints. This is a company worth supporting.

THE CONTAINER STORE
www.containerstore.com

If you need sensible storage for your papers or paints, this is the place to go. If you want to display your ribbons or buttons or other craft materials beautifully, head to The Container Store! I get all my interesting containers there. They also carry the Umbra Oh! Chair, which I've used in several projects in this book.

DOVER PUBLICATIONS
www.doverpublications.com

Throughout this book I've used lots of different images for my projects. Most of them come from readily available copyright-free images in the Dover books collection. You can find images of just about anything in their clip art series. Check out Dover books at your local bookstore or online.

DREMEL
www.dremel.com

I'm going to yell this from the mountaintops: I cannot live without my Dremel tools! Everyone should have at the very least the basic 100, 200, or my personal favorite, the 300 Series Variable Speed Rotary Tool. You can carve, cut, drill, and trim anything. It's super easy to handle and you'll be surprised how many times a day you'll end up using it. Mine is plugged in next to my toaster! Get to the hardware store and buy yourself a Dremel tool! You can thank me later.

ELMER'S
www.elmers.com
What can I say, I love Elmer's Glue-All—you know, the basic white glue you get on your first day of school for craft projects. I still use it to this day. In fact, I buy it in gallon containers because I use so much. But wait, there's more! Elmer's Wood Glue is top notch, perfect for all your building projects. Elmer's also makes an amazing spray adhesive and some terrific paint markers that you can use on almost every surface. Check out their site for all their products. You'll be surprised by what they make!

FISKARS
www.fiskars.com
They make high-quality scissors and crafting tools that are innovative and interesting. All my favorite scissors are from Fiskars. I particularly like their pinking shears and paper-crimping tools, but the list of fantastic tools they make is practically endless. They're constantly coming up with beautiful new papers, rubber stamps, and cutting tools. Make sure to check them out!

THE HOME DEPOT
www.homedepot.com
You can get anything here, from lamp-making parts to lumber. It's a great place to roam around and get inspired.

JOANN FABRICS
www.joann.com
This terrific national fabric chain has wonderful remnants at great prices. Here you can pick up lace for your spray-painting projects, felt for your curtains, vinyl for your seating, and every sewing supply you could ever need!

KENMORE
www.kenmore.com
The quality of Kenmore sewing machines is top notch, and I highly recommend their products. Even their most basic machines are easy to use and are great for all your sewing needs. They're also reasonably priced.

KRYLON
www.krylon.com
I've tried many different spray paints and these are truly the best. They have beautiful color, dry quickly, and cure wonderfully. Check out their website for all the new colors and products.

THE LAMP SHOP
www.lampshop.com
If you enjoy covering your own lampshades, explore this site. The Lamp Shop has every shape of lampshade imaginable. With a little bit of creativity, you'll be able to fashion your own lampshades for every room in the house.

MCS
www.mcsframes.com
I love frames, and this company makes the best frames around, hands down! I used large frames from MCS for my padded headboard and their smaller frames to display the art in this book. With MCS frames, sold at arts and crafts stores everywhere, you'll be getting high-quality products that will last for years and years.

MICHAELS ARTS AND CRAFTS STORES
www.michaels.com
A nationwide chain that carries every crafting supply you'll ever need. Once you go there, you'll never want to leave!

MINWAX
www.minwax.com
I finish many of my projects with a coating of Minwax Polycrylic Protective Finish (usually high gloss) because it gives everything a professional look. Minwax also makes wood stains in every color under the sun—a terrific alternative to everyday wood tones.

PLAID FOLK ART PAINTS
www.plaidonline.com
If you need lots of different kinds of paint for your craft projects, check out the line of Folk Art paints made by Plaid. These high-quality paints come in great colors and every finish. I have practically every color in my craft room.

PROXXON
www.proxxon.com
Their small circular saws, sanding tools, and even drill presses are perfect for all my crafting projects. Their tabletop models are affordable, user-friendly, and of very high quality—just right for any craft room.

RANGER DYES
www.rangerink.com
Their Adirondack Color Wash water-based dye can be used on paper, fibers, fabric, and more. It comes in lots of cool colors and can be sprayed on to create batik and other hand-dyed looks.

ROYAL BRUSH
www.royalbrush.com
I really enjoy using these paintbrushes. My favorites are the Soft Grip White Nylon brushes, which come in a wide variety of sizes and styles. They'll work with every kind of paint and provide even coverage. Invest in a few of these—you'll be glad you did!

SKIL TOOLS
www.skil.com
These are the only power tools I use for my projects. They are good quality, fairly priced, and powerful. The sanders and drills are fantastic and easy to handle. I promise you'll be happy with any Skil tool you purchase.

STAPLES
www.staples.com
I don't often get excited about shopping, but tell me you're heading to Staples and I'll be in your car before you can grab your keys! Staples is the place to fill all your office supply and copying needs. If you're making iron-on transfers, buying craft paper in rolls, or just stocking up on fantastic pens, Staples is your one-stop shop. I go there primarily for their top-notch copy center—they can do anything! Seriously, I've spent more time this year in the copy center at Staples than with my friends.

SURE FIT
www.surefit.com
If you need a quick fix for a room, this is the place to go. Head to Sure Fit for sofa slipcovers that can be altered in all sorts of ways and for plain drapes that can be embellished with anything from paint to other fabrics. This terrific company has great products at great prices. One of my favorite projects in this book is the sponge-painted curtain panels. Yup, they were from Sure Fit!

USI
www.usi-laminate.com
I could not live without my USI laminating machine. I use it to make everything from placemats to lampshades. It's wonderful to have one around—really, you can do a million projects with it! USI makes laminating machines in many different styles and a variety of widths.

INDEX